Joni Hilton

Cooking Secrets

My Mother Never Taught Me

PRIMA PUBLISHING

Published by Prima Publishing, Roseville, California. Member of the Crown Publishing Group, a division of Random House, Inc.

PRIMA PUBLISHING and colophon are trademarks of Random House, Inc., registered with the United States Patent and Trademark Office.

SECRETS MY MOTHER NEVER TAUGHT ME is a trademark of Random House, Inc.

Library of Congress Cataloging-in-Publication Data
Hilton, Joni.
    Cooking secrets my mother never taught me / Joni Hilton.
        p.   cm. — (Secrets my mother never taught me)
    Includes index.
    ISBN 0-7615-2820-2
    1. Cookery, American. I. Title. II. Series.
    TX715 .H72253 2000
    641.5973—dc21   00-050156

02 03 04 DD 10 9 8 7 6 5 4 3 2
Printed in the United States of America
First Edition

Visit us online at www.primapublishing.com

Contents

Acknowledgments

1 am indebted, most of all, to my mother, who taught me cooking basics as I grew up. My husband, Bob, a fabulous cook in his own right, has also made me a much better—and more meticulous—cook. My kids, believe it or not, have taught me as well, through their candor and honesty ("Next time we have raspberries with whipped cream, could I have mine without the raspberries?").

Countless chefs, authors, experts, and professors have all added immensely to this information, and deserve much gratitude also. Personal friends and foodies I would like to thank are: Deniece Schofield, Teru Miyashima, Hilary Hinckley, Brian and Barbara Murphy, Cynthia Rhine, Karen Rogers, Christy Noll, Charlene Royer, Ettore Ravazzolo, Jeannie Kuczewski, Sherri Hilton, Troy Hawkins, Jeanne Lamb, and my Etc. Club buddies; Dixie Albright, Aherne Del Pero, Cathi Ellington, Dara Favero, Ginger Jenkins, Gloria Morrill, Judy Ohmer, Kathy Petersen, Terry Ryan, Susan Stanley, Shelley Surratt, and Mary Louise Walters. You're all invited to my house for Thanksgiving.

Introduction

This is the most exciting time in history to love eating and cooking. Let me explain. Our grandmothers (or their grandmothers), in all likelihood, grew up knowing how to pluck a chicken, grind sausage, and put up peaches for the winter. Food was plain, but hearty. As times changed and women had less time to spend on food preparation, so too did their modes of feeding their families—meals that used to take all day to prepare gave way to instant potatoes, frozen fish sticks, and macaroni and cheese that came out of a box. Families' lives moved at warp speed and time was at a premium; maintaining an orchard or growing a garden was no longer practical, or even feasible. And there certainly wasn't time to pass on time-honored methods for rolling out pie dough, or tenderizing meat. America's taste was "dumbed down" and folks acquired a taste for powdered, instant, processed everything.

Now the pendulum has swung exactly to the middle, where we have the best of both worlds. People are returning to the comfy aromas of the family kitchen, to the delicious art of home cooking, and to the desire to prepare meals with skilled and loving hands. At the same time, they're taking advantage of the countless gourmet convenience foods that now flood the market. We no longer need to churn ice cream by hand—we can *buy* top-grade, homemade flavor. And it's the same with jams, sauces, soups, even breads. Your mom never had access to such quality or variety. (Neither did your grandmother, but she would probably have jumped for joy if she could've bought frozen bread dough.)

So now it's easier than ever to feel comfortable in the kitchen. No longer will you be daunted by Aunt Meg's home-made pesto—you can buy two-dozen varieties at the market. The fragrance of yeast rolls can fill your home without your spilling a grain of flour—or spending one minute mixing dough. Thanks to the explosion of retail gourmet food products, all the hard work has been eliminated.

And if you have your own cooking passions, you now have more time to pursue them. If you enjoy kneading your own bread, you'll have the time to because you can buy already grilled tri-tips and cut-up salad for your other dishes. If you like making pasta, jams, even grinding your own wheat—go for it. This is the time to savor your favorite cooking activities and become a real artisan in your specialties. Cooking is good for the soul, after all.

And for those of you who cook just to survive, you too can become a great cook. With this book in hand, you can feel at ease preparing great meals—you'll learn the shortcuts and basics good cooks have known for centuries. You'll even acquire new tricks and secrets to help you pull off a fabulous meal with less effort than you ever imagined. Before you can say "crème brûlée," you'll be considered a wizard in the kitchen.

Now, c'mon, Wiz, let's get cooking.

Part One

Getting Started

Chapter One

Selecting Food

It all starts at the market. In one of my recent books, *The Once-a-Week Cooking Plan* (Prima Publishing, 1999), I explain how to make an organized shopping list and I'll share this. Simply fold a sheet of paper in half three times. When you open it up, you'll have eight sections marked with creases. These are the basic categories of groceries, and you can label them as follows:

1. Cleaners, Paper Goods, Health
2. Canned Goods
3. Rice/Pasta
4. Breads and Cereals
5. Produce
6. Meats
7. Dairy and Deli
8. Frozen Foods

Keep your list handy in the kitchen, and jot down items you need in the appropriate box as you think of them. You could save half an hour every time you shop simply by using this easy method of grouping like items. When you take your list to the store, you'll be shopping in an organized, timesaving way—and you'll be picking up the perishables and frozen items last so they'll stay cold.

Generic or Brand Name?

Now I'm going to share some inside information. With few exceptions, you should always buy generic instead of big-name brands. Of course, you may have a favorite soap or salad dressing you're willing to pay extra for, but for items such as pantry staples, you'll save money buying the "plain wrap," and the quality won't be any different. (Think about canned pineapple: Doesn't ALL pineapple come from the same place? It's not as if you're buying Montana-grown pineapple. And take milk. All milk has to meet the same government standards. Paying twenty cents more per gallon for a particular brand just doesn't make sense.)

Organic or Preservative-Treated Foods

What about the difference between buying "organic" vs. food treated with preservatives? I, for one, am grateful for the preservatives that have kept my food from spoiling and will gladly continue to pay less money for this ironic bonus. But I have health-food-store friends who think I'm crazy and swear they are better off paying more for a product with a hand-written tag that says somebody in dangly earrings grew this behind her trailer (the one with the Grateful Dead bumper sticker on it). It's a personal choice, and while I will always recommend high quality and freshness, I'm not sure it has to be grown by a Virgo in a field of poppies to have nutritional value. Whichever route you choose, wash all produce meticulously—

even melons before you slice into them—to remove all dirt, sprays, handling germs, waxes, and bacteria. Better yet, if you have the time and space, grow your own produce (even apartment dwellers can grow veggies in pots). Then you'll know exactly how pests were treated, how fresh something is, and who handled it. I grew leaf lettuce in a pot once, and regularly snipped off what I needed for a salad; it was wonderful. Pots and raised beds can help you maintain perfect soil (straight carrots!) and keep pests at bay, too.

Many people believe they are healthier eating brown rice instead of white, unbleached wheat flour instead of all-purpose, and honey instead of sugar. If you prefer these items, go ahead and buy them. But just remember, your stomach only knows how to make a handful of chemicals from everything you ingest—no matter what kind of sweetener you eat, to your body, it's all simple sugar. It can also recognize fatty acids and amino acids. But it has no idea what you paid, which celebrity is also eating it, or whether it came in a recycled package.

Saving Money

There are a number of ways you can cut your grocery bill, as follows:

1. Watch for sales and promotions, then stock up on items you frequently use.

2. Remember not to shop when you're hungry; you'll just buy more snacks.

3. Buy in bulk when you can—six pounds of hamburger meat may seem like enough for an army, but if it's less money per

pound, you can just freeze it in one-pound increments. (Note: Freeze it in a flat shape for faster thawing.)

4. Purchase fewer convenience items. After all, you are paying for every step of labor involved, so precooked, prechopped, pre-anything will cost a bit more. A jar of salsa will cost more than if you buy and mix the ingredients yourself. Cooked strips of chicken will cost more than if you cook them yourself. Frozen lasagna will cost more than one you make. Before you pick up an item, ask yourself, Could I make this myself? You can save a bundle if you make some things from scratch, including muffins, deli salads, granola, pudding, cake mixes, cookie and pie dough, soups, barbecued beef in a plastic tub, chili, canned pasta, frozen dinners, french fries, croutons, bread crumbs, spice rubs, flavored vinegars, salad dressings, maple syrup—even household cleaners. (These and other basic recipes begin on p. 194.)

5. Buy fruits and fish when they're in season. Plentiful supplies mean a drop in prices.

6. Don't assume that end-caps—those displays at the end of the grocery aisles—feature foods on sale; compare prices with competing brands.

7. Don't stray from your list by purchasing impulse items.

8. Be aware of paying for parts you won't use when buying weighed items—have fish heads and tails removed before they're weighed, carrot tops pulled off before weighing, corn husks removed, and so on.

9. Check out the cost of buying rice, pasta, beans, spices, and cereals in the bulk aisle, where you scoop them into a bag

yourself and twist-tie them for weighing. You might real-
ize considerable savings.

10. Buy leaner cuts of meat, instead of paying for fat drippings
that you're going to pour off.

11. Remember that the perimeter of most markets is where
the freshest items are—produce, dairy, and so on. The further you move into the center of the store to shop, the
more you'll find processed/convenience foods—and the
prices will be higher, too. Try to stick near the edges.

12. Shop briskly. You want to take enough time to compare
prices, but don't dawdle, or your eyes will fall upon the in-
triguing packages of marketing experts and you'll pick up
more stuff out of curiosity.

13. Watch carefully as your groceries are rung up—occasionally an item will scan twice, or a double coupon gets
halved. If you notice an error, take the receipt to the cour-
tesy desk, and you may get the item for free.

Coupons

You need to be careful with coupons. Fifty cents off a major
brand might still cost you more than buying the store brand at
its regular price. Compare the net weights and the price-per-
pound signs (the fine print on the little white shelf tabs), and
you'll probably toss out most of your coupons. The exception
would be if a market offers double or triple on a coupon, or at-
taches a free product—in these cases it might pay to do a little
math before you toss out that coupon. If you really want to see
how much you can save with certain coupons, do a search of

Web sites using the keyword "coupon" or "refunding," and consider trading coupons with other shoppers. Some manufacturers even offer coupons to members of their "customers clubs," which you can learn more about on the Internet. This is an especially helpful route to go if you're adamant about sticking with one certain brand (e.g., diapers, pet foods, beauty supplies, and so forth).

When using coupons, hand them to the cashier first, then load the relative items all at the beginning or all at the end of the checkout process; you can more easily check the receipt and make sure you received the discount.

Meats

Choosing meat can seem very complicated—what do you broil, bake, braise? And which cuts of meat are most tender? To select the best value for your dollar (and meat can be expensive), here's what to do. First of all, get to know your butcher. Most butchers are happy to share their wisdom; after all, the more ways you know to prepare meat, the better customer you'll be. You can also find out when sales are coming up, which cuts are freshest, and how to prepare a rack of ribs, say.

Next, learn which cuts are tough and must be cooked longer, and which are most tender and can be prepared faster. In general, the highest-quality meat will come from the hindquarters and can be cooked fairly quickly. Usually, the more marbling of fat in the meat, the more flavor. The following are the cuts to grill, broil, roast or panfry:

Tenderloin   Filet mignon

Rib-eye steaks   Prime rib

| New York steaks | Sirloin steaks |
| Porterhouse steaks | T-bone steaks |

The tougher cuts, which can still be delicious, but which require longer and moister cooking, are as follows:

Flank steak	Top round
Stew meat	Sirloin strip
Brisket	Chuck
Cube steak	Rump roast

To marinate any cut of meat, you need something acidic (such as a fruit juice, wine, or balsamic vinegar), an oil (such as olive oil), and some seasonings (take your pick). Did you know that most commercial vinegar-based salad dressings are terrific marinades? Simply immerse the meat in the marinade mixture, and chill for at least an hour (even better, overnight). This allows the acids to break down connective tissues in the meat and tenderize it, while the oil keeps it succulent and the spices permeate and add flavor. Pounding meat also softens it and breaks up the connective tissue in tougher cuts.

★ Joni's Favorites ★

I love balsamic vinegar. It comes in many grades, and it's wonderful for salad dressings and marinades.

If you're buying a tougher cut of meat from the second list, cook it very slowly for a long time (use a Crock-Pot, a slow cooker, or simply cook it at a low oven temperature for several hours—say, at 275 degrees). Make sure you cook it with plenty of sauce or liquid to keep it moist—and keep it covered for the same reason.

What should you do about hamburger that is no longer bright red? Oxidation is what causes the surface of packaged ground beef to turn a grayish brown, but this does not affect taste or nutritive value (some people purposely buy aged meat for more tenderness and flavor). If the age of the meat is in question, ask the butcher to let you smell it, then rewrap it. Old meat will have a distinctive unpleasant odor. Solid cuts of meat will also become sticky if they're past their prime.

> **Tip**
>
> If you're going to freeze a cut of meat, freeze it with the marinade ingredients so it will marinate as it thaws.

Fish

This may sound funny (or fishy), but fish should never smell "fishy." If fish has developed a strong odor—beyond a fresh ocean scent—it is no longer fresh. It should be firm, shiny, and its eyes should be bright (not dark and sunken). Some fish are frozen, then sold thawed. This is all right as long as a) you're told, b) the process hasn't been repeated, and c) the fish is not so old that it has become mushy. Cuts of fish, such as fillets, should also be firm, bright, and fresh smelling.

Poultry

Whether you are buying a whole chicken or cut-up parts, look for firm yet elastic flesh. Look out for poultry with ice crystals in the package. This is an indication that the bird has been thawed and refrozen. Avoid any poultry in torn packaging that could allow the bird to dry out. And if you're purchasing a frozen product, make sure there are no dry, dull spots that would indicate freezer burn.

Thaw frozen poultry meat in the refrigerator, or in a sink of cold water, as countertop thawing encourages the growth of harmful bacteria.

Breads

Because of the tremendous variety available, choosing bread is now much more exciting than in years past. Don't just limit your bread purchases to sliced white or wheat—experiment with all kinds of delicious loaves, rolls, crackers, and the like. Look for herb breads with seedy crusts, unusual tortillas flecked with veggies, and breads from other countries. Fresh-from-the-oven breads are tastiest (especially fresh French bread), but you can still get delicious breads from the day-old rack for considerable savings. Don't forget to try the bake-it-yourself breads in the freezer case—fresh, steaming rolls are hard to beat! Bread-makers are another wonderful option—just throw together all the ingredients and four hours later you have a delicious loaf of homemade bread.

You really can't miss with breads, because even if you pick one and you don't particularly like it, you can always turn it into something else—make garlic bread out of it, melt cheese over it for a nacho-type snack, crumble it for stuffings or meat loaves, or make a bread pudding.

Produce

I love choosing produce; as a kid I was in 4-H, and looked forward every year to the produce display at the county fair: gorgeous, shiny eggplants and peppers, huge cabbages the size of classroom globes, carrots arranged like feathers in a peacock's tail—dreamland for a foodie.

And now you can find virtually the same quality and artistic flair in most markets. Here's what to look for when choosing some of the more commonly used vegetables and fruits:

Vegetables

Asparagus—Choose bright green stalks with tightly closed buds. The tips are the most tender, and many people cut off and discard the thicker bottom halves, but if you peel the bottom parts, they cook up beautifully. Thick stalks are most prized, but I prefer the appearance and crispness of pencil-thin shoots.

Avocados—An Avocado Board spokesman once told me to "cradle an avocado," gently pressing it in your hand to see if it yields slightly to pressure. This indicates ripeness. You can still buy hard avocados; just don't use them until they soften a little.

Beans (green)—Select only crisp, bright beans, and be sure to remove strings and trim the ends.

Beets—I use canned. Honestly, I do. The two veggies you cannot differentiate from fresh are canned beets and canned yams. But if you wish to buy fresh beets, get ones with a couple of inches of stems at the top; otherwise, they might "leak" the red coloring when you cook them.

Broccoli—Choose deep green broccoli, with no yellow or blooming florets. A tinge of purple on the florets is even better. Exciting hybrids are coming out for many vegetables, and one to look for is brocciflower, a combination of broccoli and cauliflower.

Brussels sprouts—Choose small, tightly closed heads with bright green color and no yellowing.

Carrots—Avoid carrots that are soft or dull in color. Although you can firm up wilted carrots by soaking them in water, you shouldn't have to buy them in this condition.

Cauliflower—Look for creamy white color that is free of brown spots. Make sure the florets are tightly bunched, not loose.

Celery—As with carrots, limp celery can be made firm again by soaking in water. Still, you should purchase only crisp, green celery with fresh leaves. To remove the strings, either cut an end off and peel them back, or use a vegetable peeler.

Corn—Choose cobs with consistent color and firmly packed kernels—no spreading or random kernels. Check the kernels before buying by peeling back the husks. Avoid any that seem to have toughened or dried out.

Cucumbers—Select firm, bright ones and peel any that are coated with wax.

Eggplant—Eggplants should be firm, with a rich sheen, and no brown spots. Choose eggplants that are heavy for their size.

Lettuce—Look for vivid, dark color and an absence of browning on leaf edges. A head that is heavy for its size will contain more lettuce and be a better buy. Don't pass up an unusual lettuce because it's less crispy than the ubiquitous iceberg lettuce; some delicious varieties are naturally fluffier. Wash all lettuce thoroughly (except the interior of iceberg, which is clean), as many kinds trap dirt, and will also have been handled.

> **Tip**
> Use a clean shoe horn to remove kernels from a corn cob.

Mushrooms—Fresh mushrooms have firm, unblemished, unwrinkled skin. They dry out quickly, so store them in a paper bag in the refrigerator. While dry, brush them clean.

The common button mushroom should have a tight cap with no splits revealing the underside. Mushrooms cook quickly and should be added to foods at the last minute.

Onions—Look for firmness and no signs of moisture or sprouting. Store in a dry place, not in the refrigerator. (Green onions are the exception; store these in a vegetable crisper.)

Peas—Look for firm, bright-green pods. Tinier peas will be sweeter and more tender than large ones.

Peppers—Bell peppers are the most commonly used; look for firm specimens with bright color and no brown patches. Red and yellow peppers will be sweeter than green ones. A good way to ascertain how spicy a chili pepper is, such as Anaheims, Poblanos, etc., is by size: The smaller the pepper, usually the bigger the punch.

Potatoes—As with onions, you want to buy firm potatoes that are free of moisture, then store them in a dry place. Pass up potatoes with soft spots, cracks, or signs of mold. Green sections should be cut off as they contain solanine, a potentially toxic alkaloid (although you would have to eat a lot of green potatoes to actually get sick).

Squash—Look for squash that is bright, firm, and glossy. If it appears at all shriveled, it is dried out.

Tomatoes—Yes, I know, technically they're a fruit, but we still buy them with our veggies. This is one food I encourage you to buy "greenhouse grown," even though they're more expensive. A vine-ripened tomato is far tastier than the waxy-flavored, forced-ripened kinds. Choose tender-firm tomatoes (but not mushy) with vivid red color, if you're planning to use them right away. If you want to use them in a couple of days and ripen them at home, place your greenish or light red tomatoes in a paper bag with other fruits and they will redden faster. I don't like to chill tomatoes; instead, I prefer to keep them at room temperature, like other fruits, to maintain their flavor.

Fruits

Apples—As is the case with many fruits, fragrance plays a key role. Apples should smell fresh and yield only slightly to pressure. They should be firm and bright, with no bruises or breaks in the skin. This is the one fruit I store in the fridge for a longer life.

Apricots—Select soft, unblemished apricots. If they're too hard and unripe, pass them by. You can't ripen them further.

Bananas—Buy them green or yellow (green will ripen on the counter at home), and avoid any with brown skins. Bananas reach maximum sweetness when speckled, and after that may become mushy (but are still usable for banana bread). Refrigerated bananas' skins will turn brown, but they're still fine inside.

Berries—I always turn over a carton or crate of berries to check for mold underneath. Once mold begins it will quickly spoil the whole box. All berries are fragile, and must be washed and handled carefully. Look for shiny, plump berries, and if they come with leaves, such as strawberries, look for fresh, not wilted, leaves.

Cantaloupes—As with all melons, look for firm fruit without any soft spots. Look for tight "netting" over skin that has an orange cast—too green means the melon is unripe. A sure way to know if you've picked a winner is to sniff the stem end; you should smell a sweet cantaloupe aroma. Wash thoroughly before slicing.

Cherries—Look for plump, shiny, bright fruit. Choose only the ones with stems attached; they'll be fresher.

Citrus (oranges, lemons, limes, etc.)—Select firm-skinned citrus with good fragrance and brilliant color. It should also be heavy for its size. If citrus is shriveled, or too lightweight, it may have dried out.

Grapes—Look for plump, uniform grapes with no brown spots. The sweetest ones will fall easily from the stems, and those bunches that are already losing their grapes signal the greatest maturity and sweetness. If buying green grapes, look for those with an almost gold cast; they're the best ones. If buying red or purple grapes, make sure there is no hint of green.

Peaches and nectarines—These are delicate, so be careful. Choose firm fruit, not soft or mushy ones. Make sure the color is yellow, red, or rosy; peaches will not ripen if picked green.

Pears—Choose firm pears with no mushy spots, particularly at the stem end, which would indicate an overripe fruit. If the pears at your market are woody-hard, bring them home and let them soften just until they yield to gentle pressure.

Pineapple—Tasty pineapples can be identified by two methods. One is to check for a sweet fragrance, and the other is to pull a piece of the greenery straight up—if it comes out easily, the pineapple is ripe. If the blade will not yield, the pineapple is unripe.

Plums—See pears.

Watermelon—There really is no way to judge the sweetness of a watermelon without cutting it open to smell or taste it. I thus have only two pieces of advice: Buy one that's heavy for its size (this indicates juiciness), and buy seedless to save aggravation.

Dairy

With milk, it comes down to personal choice: Those who love skim milk say anything fattier tastes too thick and creamy; those who love whole milk say skim milk tastes too watery. Frankly, you can adapt to either one, and if you have no cholesterol concerns, simply pick your favorite. Both work in recipes that call for milk. Again, all milks (and butters and creams) must meet the same government standards, so buy the most economical.

You can freeze milk and butter, by the way, if you should come across a great price reduction. Thaw it for several days in the refrigerator.

Keep dairy products cold—once they reach room temperature, they'll start to spoil and will keep spoiling even if you then chill them.

Throw out any soft products that have started to mold, such as cottage cheese or sour cream. With hard products, such as a firm cheddar cheese, you can simply cut the moldy part off, and the rest will be fine.

When buying eggs, choose large ones, as these are what most recipes call for. Again, look for value; there is no nutritional benefit to choosing brown eggs over white ones, or organic over factory-laid. Look in the carton to make sure none

✳ Joni's Favorites ✳

I love to use already crumbled cheese in recipes. Bleu cheese and goat cheese come this way in plastic tubs and make salad preparation a breeze.

are cracked. When you get them home, store them pointed-end down in a covered container in your refrigerator. You want to have the large end up because that's where there is a small pocket of air inside the shell. And you want them covered because eggshells are porous and will absorb the odors of other foods, such as garlic.

How can you tell if eggs are still fresh? Immerse them in cold water. Fresh ones will sink; old eggs will float.

Should you buy margarine or butter? Again, the choice is personal (the calories are the same). Every other year you hear that one is healthier than the other, and occasionally a cholesterol-reducing whip will come out—you simply need to choose for yourself. I prefer the flavor of butter, as does Julia Child, and who are we to argue with her?

Tip Frozen cheese is easier to grate.

A good tip when you're melting butter in a skillet is to mix in a little oil to prevent burning. Never use a whipped butter or soft margarine in a recipe that calls for solid, as the volume is completely different. And butter that sits out too long becomes rancid, so keep yours chilled between uses.

Cheeses keep longest if you wrap them well and place a vinegar-soaked cotton ball in the same crisper bin. Some of the hard cheeses come with a rind, and you can choose to trim it or not.

Ice cream is possibly everyone's favorite dairy food. Buy ice cream with no frosty ice layer on the carton, which would indicate that it has softened and then been refrozen. Also, keep in mind that the more flavorful and creamy an ice cream is, the higher the butterfat content.

Convenience Foods

A word about canned products: Never buy a dented or bulging can; this can indicate spoilage. Check expiration dates and make sure you're buying products with a reasonable shelf life. If you open a can and it makes a noticeable hissing sound (not the normal soft pop you usually hear when opening a vacuum-sealed product), throw it out—hissing means gases have been produced and spoilage has occurred.

A tip I like to pass along is to store cans upright so you can read the labels, but open them from the bottom, upside down. This way you prevent any bits of dust that may have settled on the tops of the cans from getting into the food itself. Or, wipe the top of the can clean before cutting into it.

Check the lids of bottled food, to make sure the center hasn't popped up yet.

Look at the nutrition labels on the products you frequently buy. What's the fat/sugar/salt count? You will probably be astounded at what's inside your favorite convenience snacks.

Storage

When buying packaged items such as flour, cereals, and other grain products, I transfer them to lidded plastic containers to keep air from aging them and to keep bugs out. Better yet, store such items, tightly wrapped, in the freezer.

If stocking items in a pantry for storage, be sure to mark the date—use a grease pencil—on all items. Move the older items to the front and place the newer items in back, rotating foods forward as you use them.

Finally, if you shop in a market where you can bag your own groceries, keep cold things together, canned items together, and so on, for easier unloading once you get home.

Chapter Two

Kitchen Supplies

Stocking a kitchen is both one of the most joyful and the most agonizing jobs. It's joyful because it means shiny new appliances, cool gadgets, pretty dinnerware, and having everything you need at your fingertips.

It's agonizing because it costs so much! Fully outfitting a kitchen can be a major expense, especially if you try to buy everything at once. The best way to tackle this job is by breaking it up into stages. Stage 1 is buying the bare-bones basics that you'll need to have a functional cooking area. Stage 2 is adding the "wish list" items you've had your eye on but don't need in order to survive. Stage 3 is decorating your kitchen, remodeling and upgrading, if necessary.

Essentials

So let's begin here with my list of kitchen essentials (stage 1):

Kitchen shears—These are my No. 1 kitchen tool; I use them instead of a knife. They're great for preparing salads, cutting

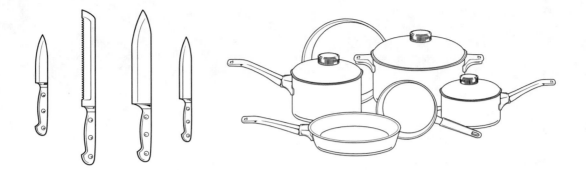

meat, and so forth. Run them through the dishwasher to keep clean.

Pizza cutter—This is terrific for cutting much more than pizza; it works great on sandwiches, waffles, quesadillas, and many other foods.

Good set of knives—Choose the best you can afford, but don't buy a dozen knives you'll never use. The basics are a paring knife, a utility knife, a chef's knife, and a serrated bread knife. I like using a large butcher knife for mincing and for many other uses, but if you're hesitant to use it, don't buy one.

Two cutting boards—You'll need one for meats and one for fruits and vegetables.

Set of cooking pots—These should include a soup pot, smaller saucepans, a large and a small frying pan, and a roasting pan.

Dishes, bowls, and glasses for setting the table—You'll need at least four of each, ideally twelve.

Utensils for the same

A drawer organizer for utensils

A juice pitcher

Set of mixing bowls—This should be a nesting set of sturdy bowls for mixing dough, beating eggs, etc. Other bowls in a variety of sizes can also be used.

Measuring cups and spoons (basic one, two, half-, and quarter-cup measuring cups, spoons to measure 1 tablespoon, 1 teaspoon, ½ teaspoon, and ¼ teaspoon)

Baking pans—You'll want two cake pans, two pie plates, two loaf pans, and a muffin tin

Rolling pin

Sifter

Strainer

Timer

Baster

Pasta fork

Tongs

Handheld electric mixer

Two or three platters/trays

Two cookie sheets

Cooling rack (or use an oven rack)

Three or four microwave-safe baking dishes (casseroles). Note: Never put metal or aluminum foil in a microwave oven.

Two nine-by-thirteen-inch metal baking pans

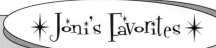

✳ **Joni's Favorites** ✳

Cutco Cutlery makes some of the best knives. Be sure to store your knives in a wooden block or a magnetized strip.

Set of steak knives

Toaster

Fruit/vegetable scrub brush

Soup ladle

Five large serving spoons

Two slotted spoons

Three wooden spoons

Three rubber spatulas/scrapers

Three pancake-turner spatulas

Ice-cream scoop

Two can openers (electric and manual)

Bottle opener

Vegetable peeler

Wire whisk

Meat thermometer

Grater (spray with nonstick cooking spray before using for faster cleanup)

Colander (with a handle)—I seem to use a lot of colanders, and I especially like being able to pour with one hand while I hold the colander with the other. A handle is the perfect way to keep from burning your hand.

Plastic wrap

Aluminum foil

Resealable plastic bags

Paper towels

Napkins

Several rigid, lidded plastic containers for storing food in the fridge

Listen to Your Mother!

Knives are some of your most important kitchen tools, but they can be dangerous if not kept sharp. I know that sounds like a contradiction, but in fact a sharp knife is less likely to slip off the food and nick you than a dull one. Dull ones also force you to press down too hard—another accident risk.

First of all, don't store knives in a way that dulls them—keep them on a magnetic strip or in a knife block with blades up to keep them from rubbing the wood. If you toss them in a drawer they'll come against dulling surfaces (wood, other knives) and may even cut you when you reach in for one. You also want to be sure knives are stored out of children's reach.

Knives last longer—and handles stay tighter—if you hand wash them rather than putting them in a dishwasher. Some knives will rust if allowed to air-dry, so it's important to dry them right away.

To sharpen your knives, scrape the cutting edge against a whetstone or a steel knife sharpener, making X motions as you sharpen first one side, then the other. Hold the knife at an acute angle so you'll get the sharpest edge possible, and always go in the same direction. I met a chef at a cooking class in France whose prized possession was a diamond-edged knife sharpener that made one knife so sharp that we all took a step back when it slid through a lamb roast with the least amount of effort. Chefs say you can tell a good cook by how sharp her knives are—well, this was one good cook!

Two or three trivets to protect your table from hot serving dishes

Bread basket (line with a linen towel, and then wrap rolls or bread with towel to keep them warm)

Four pot holders, or oven mitts if you prefer

Six dish towels (at least)

Ten dishcloths

Assorted cleaning rags (but keep them out of view)

Dish-draining rack

Vases and other containers for flowers

Candlesticks and candles

Matches

Fire extinguisher

Salt & pepper shakers

And this book, of course!

Where to Buy Them

Where should you shop for these items? If budget is an issue, consider thrift shops. Seriously, for fifty cents, you can find a glass casserole dish that you can take home and sterilize. Secondhand shops carry cookware, drinking glasses, bowls and dishes—all for a smidgen of their retail price. Scout out garage sales, too. Then gradually replace these pieces with higher-quality ones as you can afford them.

Tip
Look for a rasp in your favorite cooking store—it's great for zesting citrus and adding zip to your cooking.

Next, I recommend visiting a restaurant-supply store. This is my favorite haunt for sturdy, commercial-grade equipment that will last for years. Following that, I'd look in general merchandise stores such as Target and Kmart. Moving up (both in price and variety of choices), check out what's in your local department stores. And finally, browse through kitchen specialty shops, such as Williams-Sonoma, Home Chef, and Sur La Table. The prices will be much higher, but you'll find fabulous tools and kitchen accessories that can turn your cooking into a culinary work of art.

The following is a partial list of stage 2 items. I say partial because this list is a work in progress, as new cookware and gadgets are always being introduced. But this will give you an idea of the items you don't really *have* to have, but could save up for (or, with some luck, receive as gifts!):

Food processor

Bread maker

Fine china, crystal, silver

Extra sets of dishes for placesettings

Cake platter and dome

Gravy boat

Sets of table linens

Oversized steel mixing bowls

Standing mixer

Additional baking pans such as a springform pan, bundt pan, etc.

Cookie jar

Icecream maker

Top-grade cookware

Rice steamer

Toaster oven

Copper cookware

Poaching pan

Blender or juice maker

Malt machine

Espresso maker

Pasta maker

Additional serving platters and bowls

Punch bowl

Marble slab for making dough and candy

Silver tea service

Trifle bowl

Wok

Summer patio glasses and trays for lemonade, etc.

Soup tureen

Souffle dish

Ramekins for crème brûlée, etc.

Specialty grinders for cheese, pepper

Trash compactor

Picnic basket

Cast-iron Dutch oven

Deep-dish pizza pan

Cake-decorating pastry bag

Warming tray

Chafing dishes

Cookie molds, cutters

Additional cookbooks

Barbecue grill

Pressure cooker

Waffle iron

Two-burner pancake griddle

Professional-quality gadgets, ladles, spatulas, whisks

Meat slicer

Storing Tips

Where will you store all this stuff? When you stop to think about it, life is a bit easier if you stick with the stage 1 list, because fewer items mean less organizing and less complication. Every "extra" appliance you buy, for example, needs its own storage space or else it will occupy room on the counter and clutter your kitchen just that much more.

So before you add extras, make sure the basics are stored properly. The most important rule of thumb to follow when setting up your kitchen is to put things where you're going to use them. Put the can opener by the canned goods, the popcorn near the microwave, and so on. Save yourself time and steps.

If you really can't think where to begin, here's a good general kitchen plan: First, line all your shelves and drawers. The following four items are good, scrubbable lining choices:

✦ Joni's Favorites ✦

I have to recommend a small ice cream maker made by Donvier. It doesn't take up much space and makes enough yummy dessert for most families. For smoothies and shakes, try the hand-held Cuisinart Quick Prep.

ConTact paper, or a similar adhesive-backed paper

Vinyl wallpaper

Cushiony vinyl made for lining shelves and drawers

Linoleum

Stack plates and salad bowls in a cabinet near the dishwasher so you can easily unload them. Drinking cups and glasses should go in a cabinet near the sink (this could be the same cupboard—use the bottom shelf for glasses, the middle shelf for plates). You can stack plastic or metal tumblers but not glass, as they can become stuck and then break. Put these away individually. (To loosen stuck glasses, run the bottom one under hot water and put ice in the top one; they should expand and retract enough to pull apart.)

Eating utensils should go in an easily accessible drawer, usually a top one under a counter. Use a divider/organizer to keep knives, forks, and spoons neatly stacked. There should also be room in this drawer for scissors.

Cutting knives should be stored in a knife block or on a mounted magnetic strip—try to avoid jumbling them all in a drawer where the blades can become dull or where you could reach in and cut yourself. Some homes have a fold-down knife rack right under the counter and in front of the sink.

Cooking tools such as spatulas and wooden spoons can either be stored in a convenient drawer or a pretty crock set on the counter. Keep plastic wrap, foil, and plastic baggies in another easily accessible drawer. If you want a "junk drawer" where you can toss rubber bands, pencils, etc., use a shallow plastic container so your entire drawer won't be a mess, and then you can use some of the drawer space for other things as well—paper napkins, lunch sacks, and so forth.

Most experts advise that spices be stored far away from the stove so the heat won't ruin them, but if they're spices you use all the time, I say keep them within an arm's reach so you can season as you cook without stopping to hunt for your favorites. You can put spices in a drawer, a cabinet, or on a shelf, but I highly recommend roughly alphabetizing them. Why should you spend ten minutes looking for the chili seasoning when you could just put it near the front with the other spices that start with *a, b,* or *c?* This is also helpful for seeing what you're out of when you're planning a shopping trip.

Most people store pots and pans in low, spacious cupboards, but if you can possibly store them higher, do so—you'll spare yourself backaches lifting out heavy pots and casseroles. (Use those low cabinets for plastic storage containers, paper/party goods, and other lightweight items.)

Tip
Cut a roll of plastic wrap in half—it's perfect for wrapping up sandwiches and other lunch items.

Store mixing bowls and measuring cups with the items you mix and measure—flour, sugar, etc. This is also the sensible place to store a rolling pin, a sifter, vanilla extract, spices used for baking, and other baking-related items.

Store heavy iron skillets and broiling pans in the drawer under your stove. Baking sheets and trays can be stored vertically in a tall cupboard. Buy a rack (like a bookend) to keep them upright.

If you have a low drawer, this is a good place to store cookie cutters and other items you don't use daily (or keep them in a covered bin in your garage or pantry).

> **Tip**
> Keep an extra set of measuring cups in your flour and sugar bins to save washing them each time they're used.

Establish a system for storing clean dish towels and pot holders. A drawer usually works well, but I've seen baskets used also. You may choose to hang the ones you're using on an oven handle, a hook on the wall, or inside a cupboard door, but have a system, so damp items can dry and your counter won't be covered with loosely tossed cloths.

Wring out any sponges or dishcloths and set them neatly to dry; never let them sit soggy in a sink where bacteria will thrive. Keep your sink empty (load dishes as you dirty them).

Store canned goods and nonperishable food items in a pantry if you have one, or in cupboards that make sense—put the dry cereal near the cereal bowls, for example.

If you have high cabinets that are hard to reach, use them for storing items you don't use frequently, such as picnic supplies, a turkey roasting pan, a canister of extra rice, fine china, and many other items from the stage 2 list. Then, make sure you have an accessible stepladder, because you will, after all, use these things from time to time.

And finally, kitchen cleaners are generally stored under the sink, as is the kitchen wastebasket, but if you have a system that works better for you, use it.

Kitchen Remodeling Secrets

Now let's move on to stage 3. This is the decorating/remodeling stage, and the stage you often feel ready for within about six weeks of getting to know a new kitchen's flaws and secrets.

But don't redo a kitchen on a whim; make a master plan and live with it a while before you tackle major (and expensive) remodeling. If you have the opportunity to really rearrange your kitchen, here are the ideas I can recommend from entirely too much personal experience remodeling my cooking spaces:

Keep an old toothbrush under the sink and use it to clean the can opener blades. A spritz of diluted bleach will sanitize.

First, gather ideas and do your research. Pore through magazines and Web sites that offer kitchen design and decorating tips.

If you need a kitchen that allows you to keep an eye on the kids, choose an open plan that allows you to see into the family room, dining room, etc.

Remember that there really is something to the kitchen triangle all the experts talk about—sink, stove, and fridge should form the points of a triangle. It's a much more workable plan than putting them all in a row, or two together and one far away.

Ask neighbors for referrals of good contractors and workers. If you're doing a major overhaul, you'll want everything to be to code.

One of your first steps is designing the lighting. Make sure there's plenty every place where you plan to work. Remember to install lighting under cabinets to shine on the counter spaces.

If a bank of cabinets is hanging down over a counter, dividing the room in two, take it out. Your line of vision will now extend and make your kitchen look twice as big, and you can attach those same cabinets to a side wall if you need the storage.

Mount a microwave under a cabinet if possible in order to free up counter space and to make it eye level.

Consider how much time you spend in the kitchen and install flooring that won't be hard on your feet—such as linoleum, vinyl, and wood.

Don't install tile that can raise your floor line and thus permanently block your dishwasher from sliding out for repairs.

Get colored grout.

Don't put an air-conditioning vent where cold air will be blowing on your feet.

Don't eliminate the fan over the stove.

Install roll-out drawers in your cabinets. These will allow you to pull everything out and reach what's in back. If you have space, establish a roll-out drawer that's a flour bin.

If given a choice between drawers and cabinets, choose drawers.

Don't knock out a weight-bearing wall.

Install a warming tray where you can keep platters hot.

Don't put in an island that is so huge the refrigerator or oven doors won't open all the way. Oversized islands can block your way and cause you to take extra steps to get around them.

If you have electric plug-in outlets on the floor, elevate them so that spilled water won't run in.

Take advantage of all the great ways to store appliances—for example, in hinged flip-up cabinets, or in pretty "appliance garages."

If you entertain frequently or have a large family, consider multiple ovens and dishwashers.

A pizza oven is a cool thing.

If there's more than one chef in the family, establish workstations, i.e., separate places to roll out dough, make salad, etc.

Put a sink in your island for easy cleanup.

Build a breakfast bar on one side of your island or kitchen. Elevate it and furnish it with tall bar stools so that while you're cooking you can visit with whomever is sitting there and be at eye level (also great for when kids come home from school and want to talk about their day).

If space allows, consider putting in a diner booth.

Six-burner stoves look fabulous, but you need to take into consideration how much you actually cook: Will you really use it? If you have extra space, consider a grilling rack instead (and get the kind that vents smoke to the outside).

Make a light and airy breakfast nook, with lots of windows to let sunshine in.

A Lazy Susan rack inside a corner cabinet is a great way to utilize all that corner space.

Don't install a corner sink. They're unbelievably inconvenient when two people need to be there.

Put in deep sinks. Otherwise, as is the case with my gorgeous but shallow hammered-copper sinks, water will often spray up the sides and onto you.

Utilize tall ceilings if you have them—extend windows higher, hang baskets and plants.

Keep a trash compactor handy to crush boxes, cans, and bottles. You'll make less trips to the garbage cans.

Don't give up the toe space under counters.

If you have young children, don't choose a stove with front-mounted controls.

Research countertop surfaces and buy what you like and can afford. I thought I wanted granite until I saw how much darker it made the room look compared with another white choice. Also, the speckles on granite make it hard for me to see if I have gotten the surface spotlessly clean. And never set hot dishes directly on the counter (unless you have wood or tile), as these surfaces could crack or discolor.

Buy comfortable chairs, not just ones that match your decor. If spills could be a problem (in other words, if you have kids), opt for vinyl or leather instead of fabric.

If you are able to, make a desk space for the phone, grocery lists, calendars, phone books, files, and all the other paperwork that seems to float into the kitchen.

Don't let anyone seal your floor (wood or tile) if that person doesn't know what he or she is doing.

To make a ceiling look higher, paint or wallpaper below a high chair rail, then use white above it.

If you don't drink, turn the wet bar into a malt shop, a spacious pantry/storage area, or a dough-mixing center.

Consider placing cozy touches in a kitchen or dining room, such as a fireplace, a bookcase, a window seat.

If you want a television in the kitchen, mount a small one under a cabinet. I used to watch my husband's evening news program (he's the anchor at a local station) while I made dinner every night.

Install pretty tile on the wall behind the stove. It's easier to clean than a wall, and dresses up any kitchen.

Hate the tile in your kitchen? Instead of tearing it all out, simply tile over it.

Don't hang curtains where they could catch fire or become greasy.

If you have the space, put two refrigerators side by side. (This often requires some remodeling.) Believe me, you will use them! And two regular refrigerators cost less and offer more cubic space than one big one.

If you like to cook to music, install a music system and speakers while you're remodeling.

Use a semi-gloss paint, rather than flat, for easier cleanup on walls and wood surfaces.

Texture the "kicking spot" where kids might kick the wall as they sit on bar stools. We used antique ceiling tins trimmed with wood molding to win the battle of the scuff marks.

Consider your own personal wishes. If you want to display a collection of pretty dishes, make room for a hutch or a glass cabinet for them.

Plant herbs in pots on a sunny windowsill so you can snip them as you need them.

Don't be afraid to paint wood cabinets white. This makes a kitchen look larger, brighter, and cleaner. (I would have this done professionally.)

Stick a dab of hot glue on the corners of cabinet doors that bang shut. Let them dry with the doors open—when you close them, the dot of glue will form a cushion. You can also buy adhesive felt pads for this purpose.

Make sure your hardware matches—hinges shouldn't be in one color of metal and handles in another. If yours have been painted a different color, replace them. If you don't want visible hinges, order cabinets with invisible hinges.

If your cabinets need updating, consider changing just the doors and covering the back part to match—this is much cheaper than installing entirely new cabinets.

If you want two rooms to seem more like one (say, a breakfast nook and your actual kitchen), decorate them similarly, use the same wallpaper, and so forth.

Make room for the conversation pieces, pictures, and art objects you love.

Put the refrigerator handle on the side that allows the fridge to most conveniently open for unloading food onto a counter.

Use stud space for storing cookbooks and appliances.

Choosing cabinet doors with glass fronts will allow the eye to look farther and will make the kitchen seem larger.

What's behind your soffit space—the wall just below your ceiling? Perhaps it could be used for shelves or cabinets.

Is there a vertical space between your stove and cupboards? Consider turning this into a low cabinet for storing trays and cookie sheets.

Do you have pets? Build in a bin to hold their food (or do this in the laundry room) and an area for their dishes where they'll be out of the way.

Don't install beautiful, recessed lighting if the bulbs cost twelve dollars each.

Put an electrical outlet inside a cabinet and keep a handheld vacuum there for quick cleanups and crumb removal.

Gooseneck faucets make it easier to fill large pots and vases.

Now you know my remodeling mistakes *and* successes, the many lessons I've learned over the years as a foodie married to a closet architect. One of our kitchens—the garden-themed one—was featured on the cover of *Country Woman* magazine. We have a French-themed kitchen now (even the faucets say *chaud* and *froid*), and who knows what will follow? But the bottom line is to have fun with it and make it a room you adore. After all, where would we rather congregate with our loved ones than in the heart of the home, the kitchen?

Chapter Three

Meal Planning

First of all, no one will die if you don't plan detailed dinners with finger bowls and shrimp forks. Yes, you should plan nutritious meals that please both eye and palate, but don't get wigged out about this and think you have to fill in six courses on each day of the calendar, as if this were a job application for "Successor to Martha Stewart."

Planning meals can be much more fun and a lot less work than that. Being organized will certainly help, but you don't have to feel guilty if you order a pizza now and then, either. So take a relaxed approach and keep your menu planning enjoyable.

Nutrition

Begin by making sure your meals are nutritious. You want to feed the body and brain to keep them running well, so don't scrimp on the fruits and veggies. Watch your grease/salt/sugar intake, and plan meals that include plenty of crunchy salads

Listen to Your Mother!

Every day we seem to hear reports of *E. coli* or salmonella contamination, even in foods that appeared safe. So how can you be a savvy consumer who keeps her family healthy? Here are the secrets:

1. First rule: Keep hands and kitchen surfaces scrupulously clean, especially areas that have touched meats and poultry. We are talking soap and scrubbing, not just a wet wipe down. To sanitize your counters, spray with a diluted bleach mixture (one quart of water to one teaspoon of bleach). Don't forget to clean the can opener blade!

2. Don't let hot foods and cooked meats sit out at room temperature for longer than two hours. Watch out at picnics and potlucks—don't eat something that has been out all afternoon.

3. To be absolutely sure meats and poultry are cooked hot enough to kill bacteria, check with a meat thermometer and make sure the temperature has reached 160 degrees.

4. Wash fruit thoroughly. Better yet, peel it. Blanching fruit (dunking it in boiling water for a minute) also works.

5. Thaw frozen food in the fridge. It may take a few extra hours, but you won't risk the outer edges of food getting warm and spoiling from being placed on the counter to defrost. Two other options for thawing are to immerse the wrapped food in cold water, or to microwave it.

6. Keep that refrigerator cold! Make sure it's 40 degrees, or bacteria can grow.

and grains. You don't have to have a meat course with every dinner. If you do want some protein, think of it as a garnish to a meal mostly comprised of vegetables and grains. You don't have to eat dessert every day, either.

Appearance and Presentation

Your meals should also look good. Keep in mind that we eat with our eyes, first. If food looks appealing, it somehow tastes even better. Be aware of color and how the plate will look when it's served. Is everything brown and white? Should you add some chopped nuts or peppers to the rice? Make sure there's something green on the plate, as well as something bright, such as tomatoes, beets, or carrots. Sprinkle chopped parsley on the potatoes, brown sugar on the squash, grated Romano on the salad. You're the chef; add your signature.

✳ Joni's Favorites ✳

To make healthy fresh fruit drinks, I recommend an Acme juicer.

Advance Planning

I advise planning meals ahead of time by at least a week. Then you won't find yourself dashing to the store for something you've suddenly remembered.

Start with a sheet of paper or a simple day planner. Jot down what you want to make for dinner on each of the seven days (if you're planning meals for a week). If you want to write "take-out" on one of the days, do it. And keep in mind that if you prepare a double-sized meal, you can freeze the other half to use later in the week (freezing ahead of time is the major theme of my book, *Once-A-Week Cooking Plan*). Let's say your list looks like the following:

Monday: Spaghetti—double the pasta

Tuesday: Roast chicken

Wednesday: Quesadillas using leftover chicken

Thursday: Soup

Friday: Chef's salad

Saturday: Chinese Take-Out

Sunday: Pasta & shrimp

Fairly simple, right? Okay, look at Monday. You need something else to go with the spaghetti. (Don't forget that you'll be freezing half of the pasta for Sunday's meal.) Think of the food groups. Jot down "broccoli and garlic bread." Maybe a citrus sherbet for dessert.

Now look at Tuesday. What would be good with chicken? Fresh herbs to tuck under the skin. For side dishes, there are a zillion choices, but you pick carrots and asparagus (frozen are fine). Rice or stuffing on the side. Sliced peaches, maybe, if they're in season.

Wednesday says "quesadillas using leftover chicken"—a good no-brainer. Pick up some tortillas, a bell pepper, and cheese. Add a bag of precut lettuce for a tossed salad (use half). Make sure you have cooking oil in the pantry.

Okay, now move on to Thursday's menu. Get out your favorite soup recipe and write down the ingredients you'll need (make twice as much and freeze some for one night next week). If you still have leftover chicken, add it to the soup. Serve with some crusty rolls, maybe brownies for dessert.

Friday says chef's salad—that's easy. Use the rest of the greens you bought for Wednesday and add some sliced lunch meat and cheese.

Tip

Cook twice as much of your favorite recipes, and freeze half to enjoy later, without the work!

Saturday you're on the run, so you'll take Chinese food over to your sister's house.

Sunday you'll use the other half of the pasta you cooked on Monday (and froze), only this time you'll reboil it with some shrimp for just five minutes, and toss it in a light, bottled cream sauce. Broil a stuffed tomato and some zucchini sprinkled with Parmesan on the side.

Now you're ready to make the shopping list, as follows (which utilizes the categories from chapter 1):

Shopping for the Week

Canned Goods

Chicken broth for soup

Bottled creamy pasta sauce

Rice/Pasta

Spaghetti

Rice

Breads and Cereals

Loaf of bread

Rolls

Flour tortillas

Brownies (or brownie ingredients)

Produce

Broccoli

Garlic

Rosemary (for the roast chicken)

Tomatoes

Zucchini

Bell pepper

✳ Joni's Favorites ✳

Invest in cookware that will serve you all your life. Some excellent choices are All Clad and Calphalon for even cooking and quick clean-up.

Bag of salad greens
Peaches
Soup ingredients

Meats

Whole chicken

Dairy and Deli

Butter
Parmesan cheese
Cheddar cheese
Additional cheese if necessary for chef's salad
Lunch meat

Frozen Foods

Shrimp (or pick up fresh raw shrimp on Saturday)
Sherbet
Carrots
Asparagus

Obviously, if you also need paper goods, shampoo, eggs, milk—whatever—you just add that to the appropriate category. Now you're all set to shop, and you won't have to wonder what to fix every day.

Cooking/Preparation Instructions

On Monday, boil twice as much spaghetti as you need, and put half of it in a resealable freezer bag and freeze it for Sunday. Steam the broccoli, heat up the spaghetti sauce, and spread butter and garlic on sliced bread, which you then pop under the broiler until bubbly.

Tuesday, tuck the rosemary under the skin of the chicken, rub skin with butter (or spray with garlic-flavored cooking spray), surround it with onions if you like, and bake at 350 degrees for one hour. Thirty minutes into cooking time, make the rice. Ten minutes after that, steam the carrots. Season with nutmeg or brown sugar. Five minutes before you're ready to eat, steam the asparagus (asparagus cooks fast). Season with lemon and butter. Slice the peaches. Put everything else on the table. Voilà!

Wednesday, heat two spoonfuls of oil in a skillet. Place a tortilla in the skillet. Sprinkle it with chicken, cheese, and chopped peppers. Cover with another tortilla. When cheese melts, flip it over with a spatula to brown the other tortilla. Cut it with a pizza cutter. Serve with salad.

Thursday, make the soup of your choice and serve it with rolls. Brownies are for dessert.

Friday, slice lunch meat and cheese, then toss with the rest of the salad greens from Wednesday for a chef's salad. If you have a hard-cooked egg on hand, peel it and slice it into your salad.

Saturday, make blueberry waffles or something yummy for breakfast, since you won't be cooking dinner. Or take the day off entirely.

✳ Joni's Favorites ✳

Don't waste money on cheap utensils that will snap apart or melt in the dishwasher. The best spoons are wood—they don't get hot handles and they can rest in the cooking pot without melting. Also look for a coated whisk so your pans won't get scratched. Prestige makes a great one.

Sunday morning, thaw out the frozen spaghetti noodles. That night, place tomatoes and strips of zucchini (spray with olive oil and sprinkle with Parmesan) on a baking sheet and broil until fork-tender. Boil the pasta and shrimp together until heated through (and until shrimp is opaque if you use fresh), then drain them in a colander. Transfer to a serving bowl and toss with creamy pasta sauce. Serve pasta with veggies on the side.

Your entire week will have been a breeze—no complicated recipes or lengthy preparation times. Yet you've prepared delicious, well-rounded meals with color and variety. Now this is just one simple example of how to plan a week's worth of meals. Another week could be shepherd's pie, tacos, tuna melts, pork chops, Chinese chicken salad, then roast beef sandwiches. Or substitute whatever other easy favorites you like to fix.

You can get far more adventurous if you wish and try more complicated recipes. But starting with simple meals such as these will get you in the habit of planning ahead, and that's worth everything if it saves you time and sanity.

Timing Meals

Planning your meal so that all the food is ready at the same time really only boils down to one essential secret. I gave you a hint above, in the Tuesday menu. The secret? Plan everything backward. Begin with the serving time. Five minutes before that, toss the salad. Fifteen minutes before that, pop in the rolls. Another fifteen minutes before that, make the rice. Forty-five minutes before serving time, slide the chicken breasts into the oven. And so on. If you count backward, every course ends up hot at the same time with every meal you serve. (It's only hard if you start everything at six, hoping to serve dinner at seven. Some things will obviously be done before others.)

If you get in a bind, either keep foods warm in a low-temperature oven (wrap in foil to prevent drying out), or serve the courses as they're ready. Don't keep boiling veggies until they're limp, and don't overcook meat until it's tough. Having everything ready at the exact same second is not as important as making sure everything tastes wonderful and is served at the peak of its deliciousness.

Part Two

The Basics

Chapter Four

How to Cook Meat, Poultry, and Fish

✳

Most people plan their menus around whatever meat they're serving, making it the main entrée. I still do this most evenings. But we do know better, don't we? Meat should accompany, not dominate, our meal if we really want to be healthy. We would probably do well to eliminate meat entirely from some dinners and just eat vegetables. But if you're cooking for more than yourself, an abrupt decrease in the protein category might be met with concern, if not panic (if you're married to a big meat eater, for instance), so try to come to a joint agreement about how much meat you want to consume. Smaller portions are one good option if you double up on the other dishes. (And you will certainly save money.)

In addition to encouraging you to eat less meat than we as a country now tend to do, I also want to urge you to eat a greater variety. Studies have shown that the French—notorious for eating fats, butters, cheeses, sausages—have healthier hearts than we Americans do because they eat a much larger variety of foods than we do. This variety seems to be the key. Too many of us are stuck in the chicken-or-ground-beef loop, serving only those two meats over and over. You can be more adventurous than that. Learn how to cook several kinds of meats so that your family can draw its vitamins and minerals from a broader spectrum. You'll enjoy fixing new things instead of the same old recipes all the time, and those you cook for will find dinner-time more exciting, too. You'll find some great recipes in the back of this book.

Now I'm going to share with you the easiest ways to prepare several cuts of meat. Any time you wonder how to cook one of these cuts, just check here and adapt the seasonings you like to the directions below.

> ✴ **Joni's Favorites** ✴
>
> **Most of us forget that eggs are a wonderful (and inexpensive) source of protein. Omelettes, quiches, and frittatas can make delightful suppers, especially since you can vary the ingredients infinitely. See pp. 188–192, 241, and 247 for some terrific recipes.**

Meat Basics

Hamburger patties—First of all, consider other ground meats besides beef. Sausage, turkey, lamb, chicken—all can add variety to your grilling. Next, be sure to shape the patties with wide, not tapered edges. Otherwise, they'll cook unevenly and the edges will be far too done. Grill or fry until barely pink inside (all meats will keep cooking for few minutes after you remove them from the heat).

Meat loaf—Start with a pound of ground meat. Add a cup of bread crumbs, an egg, chopped onion, salt and pepper. After this, you can jazz it up with your favorite flavorings—barbecue sauce, Worcestershire sauce, teriyaki sauce, ketchup, Cajun seasonings, you name it. You can add bits of chopped vegetables, cheese, just about anything. I even add a splash of milk to mine, to make it moist. Pat it into a loaf shape, rest it on a wire rack inside a loaf pan, if possible (to keep the meat out of the drippings), and bake for an hour at 350 degrees. If you don't have that much time, make miniloaves in muffin tins and bake for just 20 minutes.

> **Tip**
> Add half a cup of orange juice to bottled barbecue sauce for homemade flavor.

Beef brisket—Here's a cut that needs moist heat to make it tender. Bake a five-pound brisket in a covered casserole at 325 degrees for three hours. The key is to cover it with a sauce of some kind—use barbecue sauce, spaghetti sauce, a vinaigrette dressing—anything you like as long as it's moist. Slice crosswise to serve.

Pot roast—Start with a four- or five-pound chuck roast. Coat it with flour and brown sides slightly in a bit of oil in a deep casserole or Dutch oven. Season with salt and pepper. I like to add a cup of water, juice, or cooking wine to keep it moist.

Now cover and bake at 325 degrees for four hours. Add cut-up vegetables (onions, celery, carrots) during the last hour. (Scrumptious variation: Coat the roast with a packet of garlicky Knorr instant soup, instead of flour.)

Filet mignon or other high-quality steaks— These are wonderful sautéed in butter, but if you wish to broil them, place them on a broiling pan two to three inches from oven coils for ten to fifteen minutes. Times will vary depending on size of steaks and degrees of doneness desired. There are many delicious toppings for steaks, from sautéed mushrooms and onions to fresh and fruity salsas and crumbled cheeses.

London broil—Use a two-pound flank steak and cut scores diagonally across the top. Drench it with Italian salad dressing, then broil it five minutes per side. Do not cook until well-done, or this meat will turn tough. Slice across the grain to serve.

Roast beef or pork—Get a high-quality roast, such as a rib eye or tenderloin if beef, loin or leg if pork. If it doesn't have bones to rest on, rest it on a rack in a roasting pan to keep the meat out of the drippings. Now place it in the oven, uncovered, at 325 degrees for thirty minutes per pound. Wait ten minutes before carving. (Pork goes well with apple, honey, curry, mustard, herb, orange, cranberry, peach, and onion-flavored sauces.)

Pork chops—These can be grilled, broiled, fried, or baked. To grill, place four inches from coals and turn until done (about

---

✳ Joni's Favorites ✳

Santa Maria Style Seasoning is fabulous on a tri-tip steak and on other meats as well. You can find it in gourmet or butcher shops, or order it from Scotts Food Products, Paramount, California, (562) 630-8448. Try their mesquite and lemon-pepper flavors, too.

an hour). You can also broil 10 to 12 minutes per side; brown
in a skillet, then simmer for thirty minutes; or bake at 350
degrees for forty-five minutes. A nice variation on baked chops
is to place rice and water (twice as much water as rice) in the
roasting pan first, then top with the chops
and cover with foil, so the entire mixture will cook together.

Let roasts and turkeys "rest" ten to twenty minutes before carving; they'll be juicier.

Ham—Again, bake at 325 degrees for
about thirty minutes per pound. Ham is
great with sweet flavors such as barbecue sauce, a
honey-mustard glaze, a mixture of pineapple and brown
sugar, or paired with cheese.

Roast lamb—Again, bake at 325 degrees for about thirty minutes per pound. Good flavors for lamb are mint, peach, herb,
pesto, peppers, curry—you can try just about anything.

Lamb or veal chops—Broil fifteen to twenty minutes, turning halfway through. Or, grill
four inches from coals for fifteen minutes per side (if chops are about an
inch thick). Or you can always bake
or fry (see pork chops).

If you don't have a rack to rest a roast on to keep it out of the drippings, use celery ribs and whole carrots.

Veal scallopini—These nearly paper-thin cuts of veal will
cook in about two minutes—watch them so they don't curl or
overcook. I recommend coating with flour, then sautéing
them in a mixture of butter, mushrooms, and cooking wine.

Stir-fry—To stir-fry any meat, slice it thinly (easier when meat
is partially frozen), and cook it at a high temperature in a wok
or frying pan with a little oil and seasonings (soy sauce, ginger,

and garlic are a good combination). Stir it constantly, as it will be done in five to ten minutes. To make a complete meal, stir-fry sliced vegetables along with the meat.

Using Your Broiler

Lots of cooks are scared of their broilers, which is a pity, because broiling can provide some of the tastiest flavors you'll ever sample.

Like grilling, broiling involves placing the meat just a few inches from the heat source, an excellent way to seal in the juices and maintain tenderness inside. It's a superb choice for tender cuts of beef, pork, fish—just about any meat—as long as it's at least three-fourths of an inch in thickness.

First, spray the broiler rack with cooking oil for easy cleanup. Preheat it so that when the meat touches the rack, the meat will be seared, sealing in the juices. Leave the oven door ajar an inch or so.

Tip: Transfer cooking oil to a spray bottle; you'll use less.

Also spray your meat with a flavored oil, or cover it with a coat of butter, to prevent it from drying out. Then, place it on the broiling rack (with the pan beneath to catch drippings), and let it brown. (Use tongs if you're frightened by the high temperature.) Turn to brown the other side, then finish cooking it to the desired degree of doneness.

Now I have to interrupt here. Would everyone please stop overcooking their steaks? I grew up where people grilled beef until it curled, dried out, and tasted like leather—and I couldn't stand steaks. It wasn't until I moved away and went on a date with a guy who insisted I try a bite of his medium-rare steak that I realized why steak was so popular; it was suddenly juicy and delicious. Chefs hate to "burn" good cuts of meat by cook-

ing them past their prime flavor and making them tough. So if you've always ordered "well-done," at least try "medium-well" next time, and see if you aren't on the right track.

Okay, back to your broiler. After you cook the meat, let it rest for a few minutes so the juices will distribute evenly. You'll be surprised by how fast and how easy this can be. Cleanup should be easy, too, if you oiled the pan first.

Now move on to other great broiled items. Broiling is the perfect way to finish a frittata—a thick, Italian omelette of sorts that you cook on the stove top, then brown in the broiler (obviously you'll need to use an oven-proof skillet).

Anything with a cheese topping is great broiled for just a minute until bubbly—pizza, garlic bread, a cheese-topped casserole.

And don't forget to use your broiler for cooking burgers; you'll save splattering yourself and your stove top, which nearly always happens when they're panfried.

Once you try it, you may never go back.

Poultry Basics

Wash all poultry cuts (inside and out of whole birds) and pat dry with paper towels. Remove giblets and reserve for gravy or stock.

Whole birds—A meat thermometer is the surest way to be sure the meat is cooked well enough (185 degrees). You can also jiggle a drumstick to see if it's loose, or pierce the thickest part of the bird to see if juices run clear.

Now, hold on to your turkey feathers, because here's a news flash: You cook poultry for half an hour per pound, just like you do beef roasts. So if you have a six-pound bird, three hours at 325 degrees will be just right. Before I place the chicken, duckling, or turkey in the oven, I rub it with butter and then salt and pepper it. (Try lemon pepper—yum!) Sometimes I tuck herbs under the skin, or into the cavity. Then, after a bird has browned sufficiently, I like to tent it with foil to keep it from drying out as it finishes cooking. Baste three or four times with pan juices.

If you want to stuff a bird, stuff it just before roasting it. And spoon in the stuffing only loosely. Otherwise, you risk food poisoning, because the density of the stuffing won't reach a high enough temperature. (To be safe, just cook the stuffing in a side dish, then spoon it in before you present the bird at the table.)

Game hens—These dainty chickens are fun for a fancy occasion; roast them just as you would any chicken, but for less time, of course (go by weight). Keep in mind that they are a lot of work to eat—you'll be cutting around the tiny bones.

Baked chicken breasts—An endless variety of sauces and coatings can cover a baking dish of split chicken breasts, so

✳ Joni's Favorites ✳

One of my favorite seasonings is Schilling/McCormick Caribbean Jerk Seasoning. It tastes great on a hundred different dishes. Try it first on chicken, then other meats, omelettes, salads, and veggies. It's easy to find in any grocer's spice aisle.

feel free to experiment. Bake chicken pieces at 350 degrees for one hour as a basic rule.

Fried chicken—Don't make this more complicated than it has to be. Heat about an inch of oil in a skillet. Pat dry the chicken pieces. Dip into beaten eggs, then toss in a resealable bag of flour, salt, and pepper to coat. Fry in the inch of oil over medium heat for twenty minutes. Turn with tongs. Cover and simmer for thirty minutes. Uncover and check to see that both sides are brown. Fry crispy.

(If you're watching your fat intake, remove the skins from poultry after you've cooked it—that way it will still retain the flavor, but you will have reduced the saturated fat.)

Fish Basics

Experts swing back and forth on how much fish—and which kinds—they recommend we eat. I do know this: I love fish. And so many cultures with fish-heavy diets boast a healthy populace, reason enough for me to include plenty of it in my menus!

One big secret to cooking fish applies to every variety in the ocean: Don't overcook it. Remember how meat continues to cook when you remove it from the oven? So does anything, and if fish overcooks it will be tough and dry, or rubbery and flavorless. This doesn't mean it's hard to cook fish; it just means to stop sooner! Basically, you want to stop just seconds before it becomes opaque. It will still turn opaque from its own heat, and yet will be moist and delicious.

Baked fish—Nearly every kind of fish can be baked the same way. Spray the bottom of a baking pan with lemon-flavored cooking spray. Place cuts of fish in pan. Dot with butter. Bake at 350 degrees for twenty to thirty minutes, depending on the thickness of the fish. With salmon, I add a cup of water to semi-poach the fish as it bakes.

To test for doneness, see if it flakes when you pull a little away with a fork. If it's stringy and dry, you've overcooked it—call for takeout. If the center of the fish still looks raw or gelatinous, wait another few minutes, until it's just barely flaky.

When done, you can garnish it with a sauce, a squeeze of lemon, a sprinkling of herbs, whatever. Just remember, many fish have delicate flavors that are easily masked by heavy seasonings.

Blackened fish—Don't do this to fish.

Broiled fish—Season and place on greased broiler for five minutes per side. Check for flakiness just as with baked fish.

Fried fish—See fried chicken, but cook the fish just four minutes. My grandmother taught restaurants how to make various traditional English dishes, and her fish 'n' chips was one of them. See p. 244 for this famous family recipe.

Poached fish—Boil an inch of water in a skillet. Add fish, reduce heat, cover and simmer for about five minutes. (Poached fish is delicious cold—toss with a salad.)

Shrimp and prawns—Peel and devein; simmer five minutes in either a sauce or seasoned water. Shrimp and prawns cook quickly; they're done when they turn pink and opaque.

Lobster—Boiled lobster is the way to go and there's one simple rule: Boil it for ten minutes in plenty of water, then serve it with melted butter and a squeeze of lemon.

Crayfish (or crawfish, as Louisianans say)—Boil in water for five minutes. To do it Cajun style, season the water with Creole spices.

Crab—See lobster, but simmer crab for fifteen minutes.

Mussels—Steam in white cooking wine with herbs and butter, or open them and coat with bread crumbs and butter and pop under the broiler for a few minutes.

Oysters—Fry breaded in butter for two minutes per side. Or, serve raw on ice, with lemon and Tabasco sauce.

Clams—Wash thoroughly and steam in an inch of water until shells open, five to ten minutes. Great in chowders, pasta sauces.

Scallops—Fry as directed for oysters, or bake at 350 degrees for ten minutes. They also broil well, for about five minutes until opaque. Scallops will become rubbery if overdone.

Squid—Squid and octopus must be cooked extremely quickly or they'll get rubbery (if you've ever ordered calamari and thought you were eating rubber bands, this is what happens). Quickly boil or panfry it, but only for a few minutes.

Chapter Five

Pasta Secrets

Pasta is made two ways: from flour and water, or from flour and eggs. You would think two ingredients would limit its versatility, but in fact there are hundreds of kinds of pasta, and even more ways to enjoy it. Besides the familiar spaghetti and elbow macaroni (which is still the favorite pasta type used for macaroni and cheese, and for which I've included a recipe on p. 227), there are seemingly countless other varieties, and you should try them all.

Look for colored and flavored pastas brightened with tomato or spinach. Also look for those made with whole grains. Try new twists and shapes. Each of these will offer new flavor, nutrition, and variety. Experiment with farfalle (bow tie), penne, tortellini, gnocchi, fusilli (spirals)—they're just as easy to cook, but can dress up your plate and make your dishes more interesting.

Experiment with unusual Asian noodles—there are wonderful noodles made from arrowroot, beans, and rice. Toss them with a sweet mixture of fish sauce, soy, and ginger. Or wrap up some leftovers in wonton wrappers and fry or boil them for a great new way to enjoy flavors you already like.

Couscous is a great staple to keep in the pantry and use like rice. It's actually a wheat-based semolina and cooks up super fast. You can dress it up with the same herbs and veggies as for rice. (Also look for bulgur, wheat berries, barley, and other grains to use in place of pasta.)

Ever wanted to make your own pasta? Using a pasta machine will obviously work best, but you can have a lot of fun rolling out and cutting thin strips of dough and drying them over a rack. Here's how to do it: Simply mix two cups of flour with three large eggs. Knead it (and add a little flour, if necessary) until it's not sticky, then cover it and let it rest for thirty minutes before rolling it out.

Cooking It Up

First of all, how much should you cook? For a main course, figure on serving four to six people with a pound of pasta. Put plenty of water in your cooking pot—at least four quarts. This will keep the pasta separated.

Always bring water to a boil before adding pasta, or the noodles will become mushy. Salt the water to flavor the pasta, but do not add oil. Some people put oil or butter into the water to keep the pasta from sticking, but this is a mistake—if the strands of pasta are coated with oil, your sauce will not adhere to them. Prevent boil-overs by using a larger pot. Keep the pasta pieces from sticking to each other by stirring often as you cook. Cook pasta uncovered.

If you cook too much pasta, lucky you. You can freeze half and use it later, either by running it under hot water in a colander or simmering it in a saucepan of water to warm it up. To freeze it, drain the pasta and place it in a resealable freezer bag. Label and date the bag, then spread it out as flat as possible in order to make for easier stacking in the freezer and to speed up thawing time.

When Is It Done?

An old wives' method of how to tell when pasta is done is to throw a strand against the wall and see if it sticks. Yeah, right— I can just picture starchy residue all over your walls. Don't do this; it's ridiculous. You can tell if pasta is *al dente* (tender-firm) by tasting it, feeling for that stickiness (if not done it will not be sticky), or by cutting it in two, to make sure the white center isn't still hard. Most pasta is done in eight to ten minutes.

Drain the pasta into a colander, but don't rinse with cold water—you'll lose its heat (unless you plan to make a cold salad, of course, and you want to cool it quickly).

It's all right to leave a bit of water in the pasta; if you overdrain pasta or pat it dry, the pieces will stick to each other.

The Cold Facts

One of my favorite binge foods is a cold Korean noodle dish that I have no idea how to make. I do not want the recipe. If you have it, do not send it to me. Don't even mention how you think it might be made or I will weigh 300 pounds by tomorrow.

The point is, some superbly delicious dishes start with cold pasta and are not only filling and healthy, but great ways to enjoy terrific flavors (and make it through the dog days of summer).

Once you've rinsed noodles you can mix them into a variety of delicious cold dishes. Here are just a few ideas:

Mix with Italian dressing and a jar of three-bean salad.

Mix with chunks of ham and Thousand Island dressing.

Mix with thawed, frozen peas, mayonnaise, and grated cheddar.

Mix with flaked salmon, a drizzle of oil, and chopped dill.

Mix with taco meat, cheese, salsa, chopped lettuce, and olives for a taco salad.

Mix with chicken chunks, grapes, sour cream, and curry.

Mix with poppy-seed dressing and citrus pieces.

Mix with olives, freshly grated Parmesan, and strips of roasted red pepper.

Mix with a jar of marinated artichoke hearts and a jar of sun-dried tomatoes.

Stretching Recipes—and Your Budget—with Pasta

Pasta is one of the great secret ingredients for stretching foods. Two extra people are coming for dinner? Toss an extra cup of pasta into the boiling soup. Pasta can stretch salads, chili, casseroles, vegetable side dishes, and even meat loaf or enchiladas. Not enough meat? Cut it into strips and stir it into a pasta main dish. Next time you think you've run short on some course, see if pasta can't make the magic difference. (I haven't yet figured out how to stretch ice cream this way, but you can bet I'm working on it.)

Keep the economy of pasta in mind. It's a great way to slash your grocery bill, and it makes it less daunting to entertain a crowd. You may not want to go so far as to stuff a turkey with it, but you can certainly stuff a football team, a Brownie troop, or even a dainty ladies' luncheon with some variation of pasta.

✳ Joni's Favorites ✳

I love to wear a pretty apron when cooking. I simply feel more like a good cook when I wear an apron, and everything seems to taste better. It makes cooking an event.

Sauces

Purists will tell you that the best way to eat pasta is simply with olive oil, sautéed garlic, and freshly grated Parmesan cheese. Another very simple way to serve pasta is with butter, cream, ground pepper and Parmesan. A third way is with seasoned tomato sauce. All are traditional Italian dishes.

One of my favorite pasta sauces is pesto, made from basil, garlic, olive oil, pine nuts, and Parmesan. You can whip pesto up in the food processor or purchase it bottled. Mix it with a little cream, then toss it with any pasta for a delicious meal. (Notice a trend here? There is Parmesan in all but seafood pasta dishes—but be sure to use freshly grated for tastiest results.)

Stuffed pastas and lasagnas are easy to make and easy to double for a crowd. A good pasta stuffing is a mixture of ricotta cheese, chopped spinach, minced mushrooms, and a dash of nutmeg. A pastry bag, such as you'd use for frosting, makes it easy to pipe cheese into tubes and shells of pasta.

Most popular of all sauces is the standard tomato-based sauce, and these can vary greatly. So many of us were raised on bottled spaghetti sauce that we don't always like the "real" thing—sauce with fresh herbs that has simmered all day and which tends to be a bit thinner than sauce from a jar. But the flavors are unbeatable. For a supereasy recipe for a wonderful pasta sauce that tastes like "true Italian"—but which is far quicker to make—go to p. 227.

Tip Coat your grater with nonstick spray before using, and it will be much easier to clean up.

Thicker sauces, especially meat and cream sauces, are best served with textured pasta, one with some ridges or holes to trap these heavier sauces. Also try adding seafood to your favorite sauce, especially clams or shrimp. And don't forget that pasta complements any meat you can imagine—try it with sliced sausage, grilled strips of lamb, chicken, pork, beef, anything.

Pasta Etiquette

What's the right way to eat spaghetti? The correct way is to twirl it on a fork, put the bite in your mouth, and get all the ends in as best you can. Do not keep twirling pasta until you have a glob the size of a medieval flail at the end of your fork. Twirl just a small amount per bite. And do not suck it like a straw, gathering sauce on your lips as one strand at a time worms its way in. It's okay to twirl the fork against the concave side of a spoon; this sometimes helps gather all the pasta together. Use your napkin; it's almost impossible to eat pasta without getting sauce on your lips—or elsewhere. And use a slice of bread to scoop up sauce, never your fingers.

Personally, I wish the world would get with the program and learn to cut up their spaghetti into bite-sized pieces, the way we do for children. What's wrong with this? Nothing I can see; it tastes the same, stays on the fork, and looks neater than stuffing straggles of string into one's mouth. Etiquette experts still insist on the traditional way, but I say use your common sense and keep your blouse clean. When something seems archaic, invent your own shortcuts, Toots.

Chapter Six

Baking
Shortcuts

Of all the kinds of cooking you'll want secrets for, baking will top the list. Baking is traditionally harder than other kinds of cooking; it's more of a science. Sometimes it even makes cooks want to kick their ovens or break their wooden spoons in two. Just remember, it is a poor carpenter who blames his tools. (Although I did have an oven once that—I swear—delighted in overbaking my food, and even exploded a pizza once. But that's another story.)

Unlike salads or casseroles where you can pretty much guess at the amounts and even the ingredients, baking involves accuracy. You have to measure carefully, ingredients have to be the right temperature, and you have to bake for just the right amount of time. It sounds tricky, but in all honesty, it isn't that tough to do, and I'm going to help make it easy on you.

Measuring Cups

Does it really matter whether you use dry or liquid measuring cups? Most experts say yes, but I say no. I have made gorgeous, delicious cookies, cakes and pastries using liquid measuring cups for dry ingredients, and you can too, if it makes life simpler for you.

Let's talk about the difference between the two. With dry measuring cups (usually made of plastic or metal), you fill the cup with flour, then level it off with a knife or another straight edge, and the flour completely fills the cup.

Liquid measuring cups are usually made of glass, so you can see through them. Liquids are poured in until they reach the lines marked on the outside of the cup, and you "eyeball" it to make sure the liquid comes up to the line (a thin, clear edge will be just above the line).

Tip

Using water, see how much a "regular" spoon from your utensil drawer holds. Then when your measuring spoons are dirty, you can still measure accurately.

Here are the reasons I think this whole debate is bogus:

First of all, they hold exactly the same amount (a cup of flour measured in a dry measuring cup is not a different size than if measuring in a cup made for liquids). If you're relatively careful, you can use either kind interchangably.

Second, when people make up recipes, they're stuck using the units of measurement we're all familiar with. A cake might be better with just a teeny bit less flour than two cups, but you have to write it as two cups so that people can follow your directions—after all, just what, exactly, is a teeny bit? And maybe the best amount of cinnamon is a teaspoon plus a pinch, but who's going to be that precise? They'll round it off to a teaspoon. And so it goes, accuracy sacrificed for readable, doable recipes. It's like when a recipe calls for a can of fruit—well, cans pretty much come in 16-ounce sizes, and if 13.7 ounces is what's wanted, you're asking too much of most cooks. The point is, if you use liquid measurements for your dry ingredients, you can still be accurate enough—after all, we don't know how accurate the recipe is in the first place. Granted, you want to follow baking recipes as closely as possible because huge variations really will impact the outcome. But itty-bitty variations will not. Just spoon the flour into your wet measuring cup, hold it up to eye level, and I promise it won't be but a few granules different that if you used a dry measuring cup.

✳ **Joni's Favorites** ✳

Kitchen scales are great. The brand is not as important as the function. If you have a scale, you can now use professional chef's cookbooks, in which ingredients are listed by weight.

Third, all recipes will vary anyway depending upon your humidity level, altitude, the kind of baking dishes or pans you use, how much you mix something, and the slight variations in oven temperatures. To quibble about dry vs. liquid measuring cups is to split hairs.

And last, professional bakers don't even use cups at all—they use scales, and usually metric ones. So who do we think we're kidding when we argue about measuring cups?

Bread

This is one of the most satisfying cooking activities there is— please don't avoid it because you think it's too hard. In fact, bread baking is rather simple. And there's something homey and therapeutic about kneading bread (it only takes ten minutes), smelling the yeast, punching down the dough, and pulling a steamy-hot loaf from the oven. Do it at least a few times a year for the sheer aesthetics of it, if for no other reason. And, it makes a great gift!

Here are some tips to make bread making a breeze:

Keep packets of yeast in the fridge to keep them fresh.

Use rapid-rise yeast to save rising time.

When you dissolve yeast in warm water, the water shouldn't be more than 110 degrees Fahrenheit—it should feel baby-bottle warm. And to activate the yeast, make sure you put sugar or honey in the water.

After the yeast/water mixture gets foamy, pour it into the dry ingredients.

The dough is ready to rise when it forms a smooth, resilient ball. You may need to add extra flour if the dough is sticking to your work surface—but don't add too much or the bread will be crumbly.

Place the dough in a buttered bowl, then turn dough in bowl until all sides are coated. Now cover it, and let it rise in a warm place.

When dough doubles in bulk, punch it down to release the air inside. Refer to your recipe and let it rise again if called for.

Try baking round bread on a baking sheet, country-style, instead of in loaf pans, for a fun variation. Or, braid ropes of dough into a wreath shape.

If you want to make wheat bread, start by using half-wheat and half-white flour—sometimes pure, whole wheat bread has an unfamiliar texture and is hard for some people to digest.

To give your bread a thick, hard crust, spray it with a mist of water several times while it's baking.

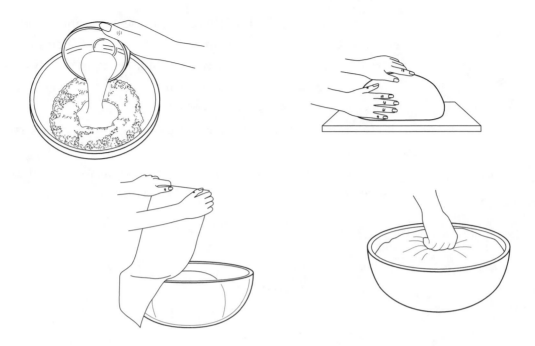

For harder crusts, use water in your recipe; for softer crusts, use milk.

Fully cooked bread should sound hollow when tapped.

When bread finishes baking, remove it from baking pans right away and let it cool on a rack. Drizzle with butter if you wish.

For some great bread recipes, including muffins, cinnamon rolls, and French bread rolls, see pp. 217–225.)

Pies

Some people claim they cannot tell store-bought pie crust from homemade. These must be the same people who can't tell margarine from butter. To me, there is a huge difference, and it's well worth it to make your own pie crust. It isn't difficult to do, but the satisfaction of a flaky, delicious crust is worth every minute. It also freezes well, so you can roll out several crusts on one cooking day and save the extras.

Here are a few tricks that will help make your crusts turn out better.

First of all, use a good recipe. Here's a delicious, no-fail one-crust recipe that you can hand down to your grandkids.

PIE CRUST

1½ cups flour
6 tablespoons cold butter
2 tablespoons cold shortening or lard
⅓ cup ice water

Cut the fats into the flour with two knives until you have a coarse pea-sized texture. Gradually add ice water, stir just until moistened, wrap in plastic, and chill. Roll out when dough is good and cold.

Second, remember that temperature matters when it comes to pie dough—keep everything well chilled.

Tip

Next time you decide to make your favorite apple pie, switch to pears for a delicious alternative.

Third, don't overwork pie crust or it will get tough and want to shrink as it bakes. As soon as your ingredients are barely mixed, chill it and then roll it out.

Fourth, if you use unsalted butter, add ¼ teaspoon salt to the flour.

And finally, use butter *and* shortening to make crusts flaky and light.

Now we're ready to roll. On a floured surface, and with a floured rolling pin, roll the dough into a circle a few inches larger than the pie dish. Fold the dough lightly in half, then in quarters, and place it in the dish. Unfold it, draping edges loosely over the brim. Don't stretch or pull it. Trim excess with a knife. You can decorate the edge of your crust with pinches, twists, fork imprints, or additional ropes of dough.

If baking the shell empty (which you'll need to do for cream pies), prick the bottom with a fork so it won't puff up while baking. I wrap the edges with foil to prevent overbrowning (tear off a large square of foil and cut a hole in the center before you wrap the foil over the pie).

> **Tip**
> **Prevent pie crusts from shrinking by limiting the formation of gluten. Use less water, softened butter or shortening, and do less kneading.**

My mother used to fill crusts with weights to prevent puffing, and if you want to do this, you can use dry beans or rice in a lining of foil to hold the dough down as it bakes.

A pie crust will be golden and baked thoroughly after eight to ten minutes in a 475-degree oven. If you're making a double-crust pie, as is often the case with fruit pies, don't trim the edges until you have pinched the top crust onto the bottom's edges. Vent the top crust with a fork, a knife, or with cookie cutouts. A brush of egg yolk or milk will give the top crust a nice glaze.

> **Tip**
> **To prevent soggy pie crusts, coat them with a beaten egg white.**

Consider making a rustic fruit pie or galette by using the bottom crust only, but instead of trimming the crust, overlap the excess onto the fruit (it will leave a large center of exposed filling).

For some tasty pie recipes, see chapter eighteen.

Cookies

"When things are bad and getting worse, keep a cookie in your purse."
—HALLMARK CARDS

Nothing seems to speak comfort like homemade cookies and a glass of milk. They're wonderful to come home to, great to pack for potlucks, and much-appreciated gifts.

If you've never had much luck with cookies, here are some tips to turn you into a cookie queen:

Never put cookie dough on a hot baking sheet—it will start to spread too quickly.

Don't grease a sheet unless a recipe specifies that you do so.

Let cookies set for a minute after taking them from the oven before you try to remove them from the baking sheet.

If your cookie recipe turns out too dry, add a spoonful or two of milk or sour cream. If the cookies are spreading too wide, add a spoonful or two of flour to stiffen the dough.

Keep cookies uniform in size for even baking.

Bake cookies in the center of the oven.

Underbake them a little for a gooey, chewy cookie.

Keep cookies soft by storing them with a piece of fruit, such as an apple. Keep crisp cookies crisp by *not* storing them with soft cookies.

✳ Joni's Favorites ✳

Use parchment paper whenever you bake cookies—it's easier to slide the whole batch off the hot cookie sheet, and the sheets stay clean!

Keep balls of drop cookie dough in the freezer to pop onto a baking sheet when you want cookies in a hurry.

Use a thermometer to check the temperature of your oven and make sure it's heating accurately.

Keep dough chilled.

Place drop cookies two inches apart to allow for spreading.

If using a cookie cutter, dip it in powdered sugar to prevent sticking.

When rolling out sugar cookies, use powdered sugar instead of flour to keep them from sticking.

If cookie-cutter dough is tearing, it could be too warm. Rechill. Or try rolling the dough out on the baking sheet, make your cutouts, then remove the dough in between the shapes. Or, the dough could simply be rolled too thin.

If cookies seem blah, consider dipping them in melted chocolate or making ice-cream sandwiches with them.

Cakes

Ah . . . the elusive, perfect cake. The reason people spend thousands of dollars for a wedding cake. Professionals know all the secrets, but I've interviewed them and now you, too, can turn out perfectly moist, perfectly shaped cakes:

Always bake cakes five degrees cooler and five minutes less than the recipe says.

Pop a hot cake right into the freezer so it won't lose moisture as it sits on the counter and steams.

Cut off any lopsided mounds—who will know?

Run a knife around the edge of a baked cake before trying to turn it out of the pan.

If the cake won't come out of the pan, reheat it for five minutes. Or, place the pan on a wet dishcloth before trying to invert the cake.

If melting chocolate, use chocolate baking squares instead of chips—they're much less expensive.

Consider wrapping strips of wet terry cloth around the outside of your cake pans (pin them in place) to ensure that cakes rise evenly. Or buy professional pan wraps.

If a cake doesn't rise, top it with mounds of fruit or frosting, or serve as brownies topped with ice cream and fudge sauce.

If using glass baking dishes instead of metal cake pans, reduce the temperature by twenty-five degrees.

When the recipe says to grease and flour the cake pans, smear them with shortening, then dust with flour, tapping the side of the pan to coat thoroughly. If using a cake mix, use a little of the mix so your cake won't have a white coating.

Whipped cream will whip faster if you first chill the bowl and beaters. Watery whipped cream can be salvaged with a beaten egg white—then whip again.

If transporting a frosted cake, keep plastic wrap from sticking to the frosting by first spraying the plastic with nonstick cooking spray. Or insert toothpicks into the cake to hold up the plastic.

Bake bundt cakes on the bottom rack.

Slice cake with non-flavored dental floss to slice it more neatly and to minimize crumbs.

To make a round cake serve more than six people, don't cut it pie-style. Cut it in half, then make slices perpendicular to the first cut.

Tip Make fluffier cakes—replace the water with club soda.

Keep cakes with perishable frostings in the refrigerator (such as whipped cream frostings).

Bake cakes in the center of the oven.

Most cakes can be tested for doneness by inserting a knife or a toothpick and noting if it comes out clean.

Fill pans and cupcake liners half full, not all the way.

If your recipe calls for beaten egg whites, make sure no trace of yolk or other oil gets into the whites.

Add final touches to the frosting with a spatula or the back of a spoon. Another way to finish the frosting is by dragging a knife across the top one direction, then the other, to make wavy stripes.

Tip Keep toothpicks on hand to insert into cakes and muffins to see if they're done in the middle—if the pick comes out clean, they're baked.

Melt chocolate and flick streaks across the cake with a wooden spoon.

Place a paper doily on an unfrosted cake, then sift powdered sugar onto it. When you remove the doily, the pattern will remain in white.

Mound curls of chocolate onto a cake—simply shave a room-temperature bar of chocolate with a vegetable peeler.

Tip

For a quick frosting, cover a hot cake with chocolate-mint patties (or plain chocolate chips). Spread when the candies melt.

To tint shredded coconut, shake it in a jar with a few drops of food coloring.

Sprinkle a white frosting with curls of citrus rind.

Be sure to see chapter eighteen for delicious cake recipes.

Cake Decorating Tips

Decorating a cake is not as hard as you may think; there are some easy ways to achieve beautiful results.

First, you want the cake plate to look clean when you're finished, so prepare now by placing two strips of waxed paper

Listen to Your Mother!

Using fresh fruit in a design (like you do for fruit pizza) is a great way to cover the top of a cake. Make concentric circles or a pinwheel pattern using blueberries, strawberries, mandarin oranges, kiwi, raspberries, grape halves—whatever looks good.

For a classic design, cover the entire top with raspberries (open end down) and a generous dusting of powdered sugar. A pile of chocolate curls is also sure to elicit delighted responses. Dust with powdered sugar for a professional finish.

under the cake (when you finish frosting it, you can slide the papers out and you'll have a clean plate).

If your cakes have risen to form round tops, cut them off for a perfectly flat cake (although many people prefer the top layer to mound). At least cut off the round part of the bottom layer so it won't rock if placed round-side-down, and so that it won't make the top layer wobble if placed round-side-up.

To minimize crumbs, give your cake a thin coating of frosting, then freeze it. When frozen, continue to pile on the frosting, and all the crumbs will stay trapped beneath the "glaze."

Use lots of frosting. You want to make sure there are no bare spots and that you have enough to work with for special frosting designs you may want to try. A cake decorator's icing recipe can be found on p. 258.

For really vibrant frosting colors, use cake decorators' coloring, available in cake- and craft-supply stores. Dip a toothpick into the paste and then swirl it into your frosting—a little goes a long way.

For a glassy, satin finish, dip your knife in water and smooth it over a frosted cake.

If you don't own a pastry bag, spoon some frosting into a plastic bag, snip off one corner (a tiny snip) and pipe frosting from the hole in the bag.

If you do own a pastry bag, experiment on a flat surface with simple leaves, puffs, swirls, and even roses (it's not all that difficult).

Toasted almonds, candy sprinkles, or crushed pecans can be scooped up and pressed against the sides of a cake if you want to hide unattractive sides.

Use a clean comb to make narrow stripes or zigzags in the frosting.

Place flowers and fruit around the bottom of the cake—use leaves, baby's breath, berries, daisies, roses.

Top your cake with something dazzling: Swirls of frosting in another color, fresh edible flowers, mounds of fruit. You can make candied rose petals by dipping them in egg whites, then sugar, and forming them into roses on the cake. Use powdered egg whites mixed with water in order to be safe from salmonella. You can also "frost" grapes and other fruits using this same method. Crushed toffee or candy bars always make a fun topper. And don't forget to try white or dark chocolate leaves (or a swirled combination). To make chocolate leaves, simply use a pastry brush to apply melted chocolate to the back side of a nonpoisonous leaf, such as lemon or rose. Set on waxed paper to harden, then peel off the leaf and stand the chocolate version on its side in the frosting with five or six others, like the spokes of a wheel.

Finally, consider taking a cake-decorating class with a friend; you'll be surprised how often these skills will come in handy.

Chapter Seven

Vegetables and Fruits

No meal is complete without the vitality and delicious taste of vegetables and fruits. Not only are they essential to our health for their vitamins and fiber, but they offer color and taste variety to jazz up our meals.

Vegetables

Everyone's worst veggie nightmare is limp, overcooked veggies that hang from your fork like seaweed. I'll show you how to keep this from happening—it's easy. First, let's talk about the various ways to cook vegetables.

Cooking Methods

Steaming—This is the best way to retain nutrients and color; simply place washed produce on the steaming rack inside a pot with an inch of water in it, bring that water to a boil, and

keep the lid on until the veggies are fork-tender but not soft. They will be bright and crunchy if not overcooked.

Stir-frying—This method also cooks vegetables so quickly that they retain their crispness and color. You'll need to add some oil and seasonings (soy sauce, chili sauce, garlic, ginger, bottled marinades, spices) and continue stirring until they're just done. Toss in some shrimp or strips of meat if you like and cook them along with the vegetables—this is great over rice or wrapped like a fajita.

Boiling—I'd give this method a rating of fair. Many of the vegetable's vitamins will end up in the water, and most boiled veggies need a flavor enhancer such as salt, butter, or a sauce. But at least the water can be used again—use it as soup stock, a seasoned water for cooking rice or pasta, or cool it and pour it on house plants.

Baking—This is a good method of cooking many vegetables that do well with dry heat or with seasoned coatings.

Grilling—Yum; vegetables will take on a smoky flavor, plus whatever delicious marinades you brush onto them. Just watch your intake of black-striped food in general, as these charred areas are carcinogenic.

Deep-frying—Though not great for your arteries, dipped into a batter or crumb coating, then popped into sizzling oil, you can get even a veggie hater to eat them.

Microwaving—This is the quickest method, and one which doesn't require the oils of other methods. Most vegetables retain their bright color, too.

Making into soups—This offers great variety and also makes use of vegetables that are perfectly okay to eat, but don't look very good and thus can be chopped up for best presentation.

Fresh, Frozen, or Canned?

I love fresh vegetables, but I'm also a big advocate of frozen ones because they're flash frozen in the fields and are often fresher tasting and looking than their who-knows-how-old counterparts in the produce section. Broccoli is an excellent example of this phenomenon. Buying frozen is also a great way to get out-of-season vegetables, such as corn on the cob, or to save time, such as when you buy an already chopped, frozen onion, for instance. Another plus with frozen foods is that you don't have to scrub them clean as you do with fresh produce. So don't think everything has to be purchased in the produce department to be good.

Now, having said that, there is nothing as wonderful as a farmers' market where you can buy snap beans that were snapped off the vine just an hour ago. Or juicy strawberries that are crimson all the way through. Or vine-ripened grapes and tomatoes. Or shiny squashes, peppers, carrots, and cabbages. I could go on and on. If you grow it yourself, or when you know it's truly fresh, there are few things in life more delightful than meals prepared with ingredients of the utmost freshness.

This leads me to why you should not buy many canned vegetables. People get accustomed to "canned taste," which is a bit salty and soft, and at times even wrinkle their noses at food which is actually superior to it. I'm not saying all canned food should be avoided (could we live without creamed corn?), but think twice before you reach for a can, and see if you can't do a little better. Of course, for long-term storage purposes, canned is absolutely the way to go. You can even buy canned potatoes (again, they have a different flavor than fresh). And many canned fruits and meats (mandarin oranges and tuna, for instance) are pretty hard to replace if you don't live where fresh alternatives are available.

Listen to Your Mother!

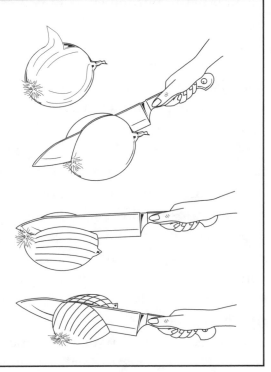

Cutting an onion is easy if you know the secret (keeping the stem end intact until you're finished). Peel off the papery parts, and cut the onion in half, lengthwise right through the stem end. This allows you to place a flat side against your cutting board instead of an unmanageable round side. Now slice through the onion in one-fourth-inch increments toward the stem, but not all the way through the stem. Now turn the onion and cut squarely across the cuts you just made. By the time you reach the stem end, you'll have diced the onion perfectly. Toss away the stem and repeat with the other onion half.

Dressing Up Vegetables

Every family seems to have a member who hates most vegetables. For this reason—and because the rest of us like variety too—here are some great secrets to make vegetables even more interesting and delicious:

Add chopped bacon.

Serve them in a cheese or white sauce, with a twist of black pepper.

Serve them topped with crushed crackers or cereal and a drizzle of butter.

Serve them with pasta and a creamy sauce.

Season with a dash of lemon or lime juice.

Season with brown sugar and butter (carrots taste especially good this way), or maple syrup or honey.

Cook veggies along with nuts for interesting flavor and texture.

Combine two vegetables in one dish.

Bake them into a quiche.

Stir them, chopped, into taco meat.

Stir them, chopped, into spaghetti sauce.

Toss them in a cool salad with Thousand Island dressing (people who hate veggies often hate all salad dressings except Thousand Island).

Fold them into an omelette.

Tip

Don't cry when you chop onions—either chop them under water (in the sink) or spray a bit of vinegar on the cutting board before you chop. Another method is to freeze them for four minutes before chopping. Lemon juice will remove the onion smell from your hands.

Stir bits into cooked rice.

Stir them into chili.

Grate cheese over them.

Most vegetables are delicious raw as well, so don't shy away from serving spears of squash, celery, carrots, etc., with a tasty dip. All of them also work well in soups and casseroles.

If you're unsure how to cook certain vegetables as side dishes, use this simple guide:

Avocados—(Although really a fruit, most people consider the avocado a veggie.) These are best simply sliced and drizzled with salad dressing or tossed in a salad, but you can cook them, lightly, in a stir-fry, too. And don't forget to mash slices with mayonnaise and salsa for a great guacamole dip. (Keep guacamole from turning brown by storing it in the fridge with the pit nestled in it; also, press plastic wrap against its surface to keep air out.)

Joni's Favorites

It's important that your wooden cutting board is at least an inch and a half thick. Otherwise, you can't lower your wrist enough to angle the knife for many kinds of cutting. And make sure it has ample surface. I like the one by Pro Chef that's eighteen inches by twelve inches.

Artichokes—Look for tightly closed artichokes. Remove leaves, cut off top and trim stem end. Tie artichoke with string so leaves won't spread while cooking. Bring to boiling then simmer uncovered for half an hour. You can season the water with lemon juice, garlic, and butter. Drain upside down and serve hot or chilled. Discard—do not eat—the choke, which is the hairy part covering the heart. The heart is delicious. A pretty way to serve artichokes is to spoon stuffing into the spaces between the leaves. Serve with butter, mayonnaise, or hollandaise sauce for dipping. To eat one, you have to pull off each leaf and scrape the soft side against your teeth—not very attractive, but that's how it's done.

Asparagus—If you don't want to peel the bottom part of the stalks, cut or break asparagus where it bends most easily. It's best if cooked vertically in a narrow, deep pot such as a coffee pot or an asparagus steamer, so that the thicker ends cook in water, and the tips cook in steam. If you don't have such a pot, you can lie it flat on a steamer to simmer. Steam until al dente and still bright in color. Another method is to bake it, again until fork-tender. Asparagus is good drizzled with butter, lemon, Parmesan, hollandaise sauce, or toasted nuts.

Beans, green—Break or cut off ends and remove strings, if necessary. Steam just until fork-tender, and serve with bacon bits, slivered almonds, butter, onions, or spices.

Beets—Boil about half an hour, or until tender. Flavor options include a splash of vinegar, butter, sour cream, or grated orange rind.

> **Tip**
> Add a bit of sugar when cooking broccoli to help it maintain its green color.

Broccoli—Trim leaves and cut into uniform pieces for uniform cooking. Boil, steam, or stir-fry, and serve with butter, a creamy sauce, or cheddar cheese.

Brussels sprouts—Rinse thoroughly to remove all grit. Boil or steam until tender. Great with butter, cheese, or bacon cream sauce.

Cabbage—Boil, stir-fry, or steam and serve with butter, bacon, ham, creamy mustard, or a cheese sauce. If boiling, the cabbage is done when it sinks to the bottom. Cabbage is also easy to grate for cole slaw.

Carrots—Slice lengthwise or widthwise; boil, steam, or stir-fry. Serve with minced parsley and butter or a sweet glaze. If putting carrots around a roast, boil them for a few minutes first, so they'll be tender when finished roasting.

Cauliflower—See broccoli.

Celery—Slice crosswise at a diagonal and stir-fry, boil, or steam. Great with buttered carrots.

Corn—After stripping off husks and silk, boil with a dash of sugar in the water to bring out the corn's sweetness. Or grill for twenty minutes, brushed with a spicy marinade.

Cucumber—We're so used to seeing this in salads, or pickled, that we don't often remember it can be cooked quite successfully, too. Simply peel, slice thinly, and steam. Serve with butter or cream sauce.

Eggplant—Fry, bake, boil—you name it. Eggplant is good with mozzarella cheese and spaghetti sauce, or served with bacon.

Slice it and dip into egg, then flour, for a coating before you fry it. Fry quickly, as eggplants are like sponges and will absorb much of the oil if the oil isn't hot enough. Some eggplants have a bitter quality, which can be removed by sprinkling the eggplant with salt, letting it rest for fifteen minutes, then rinsing before proceeding with your favorite recipe. Mine is ratatouille, a wonderful stew of diced eggplant, zucchini, onion, tomato, peppers, and garlic.

Lettuce—Usually you'll serve it in a salad, but don't discount the idea of using it as a wrap for rice/sausage/veggie mixtures. Store it wrapped in a paper towel on the bottom of the crisper so it won't get mushy.

Mushrooms—Great for topping steaks. Sauté sliced or whole for just a couple of minutes in a mixture of butter and Worcestershire sauce. Also an excellent choice for a stir-fry mixture, but add the mushrooms last.

Onions—Peel and slice. Boil, fry, stir-fry, bake, steam—onions are versatile. I love them simply with butter, but many people enjoy them most when mixed with another vegetable, or served with a cream sauce. And don't forget onion soup!

Peas—Peas cook quickly, so check them frequently. Boiling is fine; then drain and serve with butter, mushrooms, onions, or a myriad of spices, including mint and curry. (Try some of the new spice blends in shaker bottles in the spice aisle.)

Peppers, bell—Cut open to remove seeds and membrane. They can be cooked any way you can imagine except by boiling, which will dull their color. To make stuffed peppers, cut off the tops and parboil them for five minutes, then stuff them with a tasty rice pilaf and bake until tender. Peppers are good tossed with other veggies to spice them up, and they're also great sliced—raw—into strips. But my favorite way to enjoy peppers, roasted, really brings out the sweet flavor of this vegetable. You can roast them yourself or buy roasted red peppers in a bottle at the market (much easier).

✳ Joni's Favorites ✳

For chopping veggies that you'll use to make soup, you can't beat the Braun Blender.

Potatoes—Now we are talking endless variety. There are probably as many ways to prepare potatoes as there are potatoes. You can cut them up, boil them, drain them and mash them with some sour cream and butter. (If boiling potatoes for salad or mashed potatoes, dice them first for faster cooking.)

Or, you can slice them into strips and fry them in oil. (When frying, put a metal colander upside down over the frying pan to allow air to circulate while catching spatters.) Or you can grate them and make hash browns. You can also bake them and serve them with various toppings. (Potatoes will bake faster if you skewer them with a metal shish-kebab skewer—the metal will conduct heat to the centers.) Or, boil new red potatoes and serve them with garlic butter. Or make scalloped potatoes by slicing them and baking in a cream sauce. To keep sliced potatoes from darkening, keep them immersed in water. To bake a potato with a crisp skin, rub it with butter, then pierce several times with a fork to vent. Place directly on the oven rack and bake.

Tip Store an apple with your potatoes to keep them from sprouting roots.

Squash—See eggplant.

Spinach—Discard stems; serve raw as salad. Or, to cook, rinse thoroughly and place in dry pot, with water still clinging to leaves. Heat to medium and spinach will steam and wilt as it should with just the water on the leaves. Spinach is good with butter, bacon, chopped boiled egg, vinaigrette, onion, and cheese flavors.

Tomatoes—Stewed, fried, stuffed, and baked—tomatoes are available all year and add color to any meal. To stuff, remove stem ends and scoop out pulp. Fill with a mixture of crushed croutons and grated Parmesan. Bake twenty minutes at 350 degrees. To stew, peel them and mix with chopped onion, a bit of sugar, salt, and pepper, and simmer in a saucepan for ten minutes. (Peeling tomatoes is easy if you first blanch them by immersing them in boiling water briefly.)

Yams and sweet potatoes—Peel and slice, then bake, fry, or boil, just as you would a standard potato. Yams are wonderful with butter and brown sugar, or baked along with apples in a sweetened sauce. And a slice of sweet potato pie never hurts.

Listen to Your Mother!

Ice-cube trays are one of the handiest little containers in the kitchen, and not just for ice. If you use them to freeze other foods, you can then transfer the frozen cubes to resealable freezer bags and have small portions whenever you like.

Here are some great things to freeze in small increments:

Herbs in broth, for adding to soups and stews

Whipped cream

A paste of two tablespoons butter and two tablespoons flour for making white sauce (heat with a cup of milk, salt, and pepper)

Juice—when you use the cubes in drinks, you won't dilute the drinks

Cookie dough for big, monster cookies

Mashed fruit for making smoothies in the blender

Mashed bananas for making banana bread

Spaghetti sauce for when you need only one or two servings

Hamburger for making uniform meatballs

Mashed potatoes (which are a great thickener for soups and gravies)

Pie dough

Cooked, pureed veggies for adding to soups or feeding to baby

Fruits

I'm always disappointed when people serve fruit for dessert. My taste buds run strong, and except for pineapple and melons, fresh fruit is almost always too sour for me. (Serve a fruit pie, however, and now we're talking.)

Nevertheless, I know fruit is an excellent, healthy snack choice, as well as a great way to enjoy something sweet without added sugar and fats. But did you know that fruits can also be cooked and enjoyed as accompaniments to your dinner menu? They're a great way to get more vitamins into your family and to spark up a too-familiar meal. Try these suggestions next time you feel like fixing something new for dinner:

Apples—Don't let apples sit in your fruit basket or fridge until they get soft and wrinkly. If nobody's eating them, make applesauce. Peel and dice them, and stir over low heat to release their juices. Season with cinnamon and brown sugar. For apple pies, use Granny Smith, Empire, or pippin apples. To bake them, use Rome Beauty apples, as they hold together best.

Tip
Core apples quickly with a melon baller.

Apricots—Whether dried or fresh, minced apricots add bright color to rice pilafs, stuffings, cakes, or cookies. Tiny apricot tarts are a delicious delicacy.

Bananas—Besides eaten fresh, bananas can be stewed in butter for a delicious side dish that is popular in Latin regions. They work marvelously in pies and breads and can become a terrific topping for ice cream if cooked with brown sugar and pecans.

Berries—We all know berries are wonderful with jams, pies, cheesecakes, and ice cream, but they're also delightful in green salads, especially with a sweet salad dressing. Or serve them dusted with powdered sugar and splashed with whole cream.

Cantaloupe—Truly fragrant, ripe cantaloupe is best served fresh, as is. But one delicious option is to wrap small chunks of it with prosciutto ham and serve it as an appetizer. The salty flavor of the meat goes perfectly with the sweet melon.

Cherries—Pit cherries and use them in stews or to enhance the flavor of meats such as duckling or pork. They're also delightful in a cold salad, or minced and mixed into candy filling or cookie dough.

Citrus—Use juices and zest liberally to season everything from cakes to roast chicken. Stewed orange segments, in a sweet sauce, are also delicious.

Grapes—Grapes are most commonly served fresh, but you can bake them along with chicken or fish in a light white wine sauce to make a *Véronique*. Grapes are also a wonderful accompaniment to a selection of cheeses.

Peaches—Peach jam is wonderful to spread over a pork roast before baking. But peach desserts really showcase this gorgeous fruit: Try cobblers, sorbets, pies, and cakes. Also great with raspberries.

Pears—Poached, sliced into a tart, chopped into a salsa, or pureed to replace half the oil in baked goods, pears are an excellent surprise to most diners. Their flesh and flavor are both more delicate than that of apples, but they can often be substituted for apples in most any recipe. Pears are especially good in a green salad with candied nuts and a sharp *bleu* cheese.

Pineapple—Slice and bake with butter and brown sugar for a colorful, sweet side dish. Pineapple goes especially well with ham and fish. Chop it up with some diced red onion and cilantro for a tropical salsa. Or make a terrific salad: Dice it and toss with leaves of romaine and poppy-seed dressing.

Tip: Use a vegetable peeler to peel apples and pears—you'll lose less of the fruit than if you use a paring knife.

Plums—See cherries.

Watermelon—How can you improve upon the taste of fresh watermelon? Simply slice it and serve, and be glad it's in season.

Salads

Everyone should know how to make a good salad—and I don't just mean torn-up lettuce and a bottled dressing. You can make a knockout salad and a good vinaigrette that will see you through many a dinner party. Here's a good, basic vinaigrette:

BASIC VINAIGRETTE

1 cup olive oil
⅓ cup balsamic vinegar
2 teaspoons crushed basil leaves
1 teaspoon crushed garlic
½ teaspoon dry mustard
salt and pepper to taste

To get the mixture to form an emulsion, either whisk it vigorously, shake it in a jar, or whip it in a blender. Cover and store in the refrigerator.

You can make variations on your vinaigrette by adding bacon bits, mayonnaise, feta cheese, chopped sun-dried tomatoes, olives, grated Parmesan cheese, fruit, sesame seeds, pureed berries, or a myriad of other ingredients.

Now, what do you put it on, if not torn-up lettuce? Well, you start with the lettuce— a mixture of kinds if possible. For faster cutting, use shears instead of tearing it or using a knife.

Discard woody stems and thick pieces. If you need to dry rinsed salad leaves and you don't have a salad spinner, put the pieces in a clean pillowcase and spin-dry it in your washing machine. If using packaged salad greens, sort through them and discard any which look limp or brown-edged.

Then, vary the other ingredients as you like, taking care to use lots of bright color (tomatoes, carrots, purple cabbage, red onion, mandarin oranges, blueberries, papaya, yellow squash) and interesting textures (nuts, cheeses, crunchy jicama or water chestnuts, croutons). Toss with cooked seafood or chicken for a main-dish salad. Some easy but delicious salad recipes begin on p. 232.

Tip

Easily remove the core from a head of iceberg lettuce by hitting the stem on the corner of your counter. The core should pull right out.

Chapter Eight

Flavoring Your Food

t he best flavors in the world are the natural flavors of the foods themselves. Rather than mask these, this chapter will show you how to bring them out, enhance them, and make them even more delicious to a wider audience.

Oils

Whenever you eat something that seems tasteless or dry, oil is probably the missing ingredient. And though we all want to watch our intake of saturated fat, you have to use some kind of fat medium to cook many of the dishes you enjoy. Even if you substitute pureed fruit for half the oil or butter in baked goods (a good way to cut down on fat), you still need some oil, both for moisture and flavor.

Cutting Back

Oils range from lard and butter (both animal fats) to olive, corn, and soy oils, which come from plants. I am guilty of cooking with too much butter and cream, but I try to make up for it by removing the skin from chicken, drinking skim milk, and using canola oil instead of high-cholesterol oils.

If you're trying to cut down on saturated fat but you love all the wrong foods, try this: Instead of attempting to live completely without chips, desserts, donuts, fried chicken, etc., make your portions smaller. Consider yourself a "taster," and fill up on crisp vegetables while still indulging in an occasional bite or two of your favorites. Remind yourself that you do not need to eat the whole thing to experience it. Share an order in restaurants, splitting it with your spouse or a friend. Or ask for a doggie bag and take half home for another meal.

Margarine or Butter?

The debate rages on. For a time, butter was the bad guy, but now scientists are saying that the process of making margarine turns some of the unsaturated fat into transfatty acids and we're just as well off to eat butter in the first place. Whipped spreads, oil-based spreads, and even ones that promise they have no cholesterol at all are available for the trying. Just don't substitute a whipped spread for a solid butter or margarine when baking, as soft products contain different amounts of air and water and will throw off your recipe.

Shortening

Many experts shun the use of what we consider shortening—canned fluff that greases our cake pans and moistens our cookie dough. But I like it; it's soft and easy to work with, and it's made from vegetable oil (although it is hydrogenated, the same process used for margarine that I spoke about above). It even comes in a butter flavor for those who miss that buttery taste. Purists (i.e., Europeans) scorn those of us who use it, but then again, *I* drink skim milk.

Lard?

I have a brick of it in my refrigerator. I know, this makes the average person gasp and fall speechless. It's the same way I react to people who go out in the sun without wearing sunscreen—don't they read the papers? Don't they know the health risks? Okay, but I am not slathering lard on my English muffins in the morning; I am using it strictly for pie dough, and even then I use both lard and butter. The reason for this lies in the results; somebody else's golden tan is my flaky pastry. You simply cannot get flakier pie crusts than those made with at least a smidgen of lard. So there it sits, heavy and greasy. And, well, wonderful.

✳ Joni's Favorites ✳

A great blend of olive and canola oil (so the olive oil doesn't taste quite so strong when cooking with it) is made by Marcos and available in ethnic markets.

Drippings

I do not advise saving drippings. If you want to use them right away, do so; they are wonderful for gravies, sauces, stews, and much more. But too often drippings are stored improperly, become rancid, or get mixed with other drippings. And, frankly, they're pure animal fat, so they're not good for you. If you want to flavor something with bacon or another meat, cook it up fresh when you want the flavoring.

Frying with Oil

Right off the bat, we should all fry less. If given a cooking choice, we shouldn't opt for dropping everything in sizzling oil but rather steaming, poaching, and seasoning with herbs whenever possible. Nevertheless, there will be occasions when you'll want to fry up some funnel cakes, fries, wontons, fritters, chicken, or a dozen other tasty treats, and I'm going to share a couple of little-known tips that will help ensure your success.

Tip

If coating, say, chicken pieces with flour for frying, the flour will adhere better if you chill the chicken for half an hour after you coat it.

The main secret is to heat the oil to the right temperature—oil should be extremely hot, so it doesn't get absorbed by the food, but not hot enough to start smoking (oil can also catch fire). To see if the oil is hot enough, drop in a pinch of bread and see if it sizzles and fries crispy. If it stays mushy or sinks to the bottom, the oil isn't hot enough. With practice, you can also test oil by flicking a few drops of water into it and seeing if they pop and sizzle.

Seeing to it that the food pieces are the same size so they'll cook evenly is another important element of frying. This is obviously impossible with chicken pieces, but if you're frying donuts, fish segments, and so on, cut them all as uniformly as possible.

Fried foods have one distinct disadvantage from a taste standpoint: They must be eaten while fresh and hot, or they sink heavily into your stomach, dense, greasy and seemingly non-biodegradable. If you're serving fried foods to guests, wait until they arrive before frying things up, or you could find yourself with a soggy, limp entrée—and a greasy stove top to clean, to boot.

Old vs. New Oil

Many cooks strain and reuse oil several times before discarding it, but I don't like the residual flavors oil holds, so my advice is to toss it out after using it. This is a more expensive way to go, but perhaps it will keep you from frying as often!

Flavored oils have hit the market in a big way, and they're wonderful for infusing food with delicious spices and herbs. They're especially fun in salad dressings, and even look pretty sitting on the counter with a sprig of rosemary or with a bright pepper inside a tall bottle. Incidentally, oil is wonderful for preserving garlic—drop a peeled clove into a jar of oil, and not only will it keep the garlic from spoiling, but you'll have delicious garlic oil to use next time you have a fish fry.

Marinades

A marinade is a mixture of three basic things: Oil, to keep meat succulent; something acidic such as lemon, vinegar or wine, to break down the connective tissues and tenderize it; and seasonings to add flavor. You can find all three in a bottle of Italian salad dressing, or in many of the bottled marinades now on the market, from Cajun to Asian. Whisk the ingredients together vigorously so they won't separate. Meats are soaked in this liquid, covered and in the refrigerator so they won't spoil, for anywhere from twenty minutes to overnight. Usually you'll want to turn the meat at least once so that both sides make contact with the mixture. Then, when the meat is cooked, it's infused with moisture, flavor, and tenderness.

Tip: Use a rubber jar-opener pad to remove skins from garlic.

Many marinade recipes advise brushing additional marinade onto the meat while it cooks.

You can make your own marinades as long as you use an acid, an oil, and some flavorings. The amounts are not critical; just splash on the liquids and toss on the herbs! Here are some great ones to try—they work on beef, chicken, fish, or pork:

Barbecue sauce and crushed pineapple

Any noncreamy salad dressing

Worcestershire sauce, soy sauce, and vegetable oil

Balsamic vinegar, olive oil, basil, oregano, garlic

Orange juice, brown sugar, oil, rosemary

Lemonade, vegetable oil, lemon pepper

Tomato juice, olive oil, basil, and oregano

Lime juice, garlic-flavored oil, chopped cilantro, red pepper flakes

Apricot nectar, oil, chili flakes

Russian dressing and a package of instant onion soup

Balsamic vinegar, vegetable oil, mustard, honey

Cranberry juice, vegetable oil, orange zest, sage

Tahini sauce, for a Middle Eastern twist

Thai fish sauce, chili oil, ginger

White grape juice, vegetable oil, curry

Cider vinegar, vegetable oil, maple syrup, cloves

Chili sauce and vegetable oil

Any chutney and garlic oil

✳ Joni's Favorites ✳

Extra virgin olive oil—so heart healthy, and so delicious. I like the one by Il Fornaio.

Salsa, vegetable oil, chopped olives

Hoisin sauce, sesame oil, sugar

Teriyaki sauce, oil, chopped mango or pineapple, sugar

Rice vinegar, sesame oil, crushed garlic

You need not limit your ingredients to three; these are just basic starting places. Mix in some minced onion, chopped tomatoes, capers, thyme, paprika, chili peppers—whatever you wish—to add even more interest to these marinades.

One of the great things about marinating is that you can prepare your dinner the night before, let it marinate all day while you're at work, and have a scrumptious, unhurried-tasting meal that night, by just popping it into the oven or microwave.

You can also marinate chunks of beef before you stew them, chicken before you fry it, even ground beef before you make hamburgers, for a delightful taste surprise.

If you hit upon a favorite marinade, make up a bottle of it and keep it in the fridge so it will be handy—you can even brush it onto grilled vegetables.

Flavorings and Extracts

Every good cook has vanilla extract in her pantry and usually a few other goodies for adding flavor to all kinds of baked goods. I keep an assortment of extracts I use for ice cream and candy making, but they can also liven up savory foods such as soups, sauces, and meats. Just be

Tip

Is a sauce too sweet? Add a dash of cider vinegar.

cautious in using them; some impart a "fake" citrus flavor or a toothpastey "mint" flavor. Next time you're ready to use vanilla, try raspberry or almond extract for a change of pace.

Savory flavorings, such as Liquid Smoke, add a grilled flavor to oven-barbecued foods, and bouillon cubes are indispensable for providing richness to soups and sauces. Consider butter-flavored sprinkles if you really want to cut fats.

Herbs and Spices

Spend time browsing in the seasonings aisle. Not only will you find all the familiar spices you grew up with, but you'll also discover a seemingly endless array of spice blends made just for steaks, just for fish, or for capturing the ethnic tastes of exotic places. Look for spice rubs and blends in Caribbean, Latin, Cajun, East Indian, Mediterranean, Asian, and Middle Eastern flavors. Just one shake of these in a pot of rice or pasta can make it come alive and taste like a complicated recipe.

Freshly ground spices are always noticeably better, but we can't all keep up with drying and grinding every herb and bulb when we need their flavors, so it's okay to stock your spice shelf with the convenience of the dried kind. (You may, however, want to choose a few that you always get in the produce department and grate fresh, such as ginger or nutmeg, and ones you chop fresh, such as basil or rosemary.)

Here are the basic herbs and spices to have on hand, and what to put them on:

Allspice—This is not actually a mixture of "all spices" but one kind of plant, called the allspice. Use it on fish and poultry, roasts, squash, spice cakes, pumpkin pies.

Anise seeds—Licorice flavored, these add a sweetness to curries, fish dishes, baked goods.

Basil—This is great with any Italian or tomato-based sauce, on fish, in green salads, with mozzarella cheese, in omelettes. Wrap shrimp in whole leaves and skewer for roasting.

Bay leaves—These add a great fragrance to soups and stews, but remove them before serving (dried bay leaves have such sharp edges they can actually cut your mouth).

Caraway seeds—Best in cabbage dishes such as cole slaw.

Cayenne pepper—Also known as red pepper, it is very concentrated, so use sparingly.

Chili powder—Pep up meat loaf, chili (of course), cheese sauces, barbecue, potatoes, and corn.

Cilantro—It's hard to imagine any Southwestern dish without cilantro. Buy it fresh and snip it up. Also a great addition to Asian and Mediterranean dishes.

Cinnamon—Fabulous for cinnamon rolls and quick breads, but also good with carrots, ham and pork, chicken and shrimp.

Clove—Strong, so be careful. Use with fish, chicken, ham, orange vegetables, onions, fruit sauces, baked goods.

Cream of tartar—This is essential when making meringues, angel food cakes, and stiff frosting. You can also make baking powder out of it—mix ½ teaspoon of it with ¼ teaspoon

* Joni's Favorites *

Buy herbs fresh or grow a few in a sunny windowsill. It's a joy to snip your own fresh herbs into a wonderful dish you prepare. The most commonly used herbs are basil, Italian flat-leaf parsley, thyme, oregano, chives, rosemary, marjoram, cilantro, and tarragon.

cornstarch and ¼ teaspoon baking soda. Cream of tartar is an interesting by-product of the wine-making process.

Cumin—Very hot, so be careful. Used in savory dishes, rice, and meats from Africa, Spain, Mexico, and India.

Curry powder: Associated with Indian dishes, this sweet flavoring (actually a blend of spices) can also become spicy-hot if used in great quantity. Even a small dash of it will give a greenish—but delicious—cast to oils, rice dishes, cream sauces, salads, and meats.

> **Tip**
>
> To calm the fire in a spicy dish, stir in sour cream or yogurt (or drink plenty of milk).

Dill—Best with fish, dill is also great in potato salads, green salads, or sprinkled on just about any vegetable or rice dish.

Fennel—This slightly licorice-flavored herb is wonderful in Italian dishes and cooked vegetables.

Ginger—Good with all kinds of meat, ginger gives an Asian flair to soups and salads; it's also wonderful in baked goods.

Lemongrass: Buy this fresh, then peel and chop for a marvelous flavor and aroma in any Asian dish.

Mace—This aromatic spice enhances soups and stews, especially those that are poultry and fish based. Good on the broccoli family of vegetables, and in creamy custard-type desserts.

Marjoram—It's terrific in any soup or gravy; with any meat, particularly lamb; with tomato-based dishes; with cooked greens and fresh salads.

Mustard—Dry mustard is superb for adding pungent flavor to such mixtures as barbecue sauce, cream sauces, and stews.

Nutmeg—This is wonderful grated into soups, stews, roast dishes, beans, carrots, pies, and quick breads.

Oregano—Common in Italian dishes such as pizza and spaghetti, oregano is also terrific with any meat, kneaded into bread dough, tossed with a salad dressing, stirred into a dip or spread. Very strong, so use a light touch.

Paprika—Mildly spicy and a bit sweet, this ground pepper is a seasoning found in almost any savory dish. Most of us have seen it sprinkled over potato salad as a garnish.

Parsley—There is no need to buy this dried when it's always available fresh and can be quickly snipped up with shears. Parsley can add flavor to almost any meat, vegetable, or salad, and is a pretty garnish, too.

Poppy seeds—Good in salad dressings and in poppy-seed baked goods, such as cakes and breads.

Tip

Remove fat from a gravy-based dish by chilling it with plastic wrap touching the surface—the fat will harden and peel right off with the plastic.

Rosemary—Fragrant and French, wonderful with any meat.

Saffron—Extremely pricey, saffron is mostly used to create brilliant yellow coloring. Excellent in rice or broths.

Sage—Best with poultry, stuffings, biscuits, hearty soups.

Sesame seeds—Pretty and nut flavored, sesame seeds are great tossed into salads and Asian stir-frys, and pressed on top of rolls and breads.

Summer savory—Good in stews, but even better kneaded into bread dough.

Tarragon—This is my favorite spice. It's wonderful in cream sauces, with eggs, made into a Bernaise sauce, or served with any meat or fish, particularly salmon (my favorite fish).

Thyme—Excellent in fish and poultry dishes, chowders, with veggies (try it on french fries), and cheese-based dishes.

Turmeric—Used mainly in Indian dishes, turmeric has a harsh flavor and a bright yellow tint.

Vanilla—In its liquid extract form, vanilla is indispensible for making desserts. For vanilla-scented sugar, keep fresh vanilla beans in a jar of sugar.

White pepper—It's perfect for spicing up white foods—cream sauces, light gravies, seasoned butters—anything where you don't want dark flecks to show.

When used properly, spices can contribute so much flavor that they can actually help you reduce the fats in many foods. Have fun experimenting with new flavors and combinations!

Part Three

Helpful
Hints

Chapter Nine

Freezing Leftovers

believe me, you will want to freeze leftovers. Even if you are a person who hates leftovers, you will want to:

Save money

Save time

Save cleanup hassle

Save thinking of what to have for dinner

You can do all of that—it just takes planning.

Deliberate Leftovers

Every time you make a dish such as a soup, a casserole, or anything except a green salad, make double the amount. Plan to freeze half, and tuck it away for sometime next week.

In my book *The Once-a-Week Cooking Plan* (Prima Publishing, 1999), I advocate going even further and cooking just once each week so that every day is taken care of, labeled, and frozen. Then, the first person home simply pops that day's meal into the oven. It's a great way to simplify your life and free up more time. The book also outlines shopping lists and menus to make it a slam dunk.

But, you can also benefit from simply cooking in batches and doubling most recipes. Freeze a dozen extra rolls, leftover pasta, rice, or mashed potatoes, and all you'll need is a quick salad to go with your main course.

It also pays to freeze commonly used ingredients. Let's say you often make entrees that call for cooked ground beef and onions, or cooked shredded chicken. Doesn't it make sense to cook up a giant batch, then freeze in recipe-sized increments? Later, when you want some seasoned beef for a lasagna, the messiest part is already done. Doing this has saved me countless hours when I need to throw together a quick meal. Bacon bits are another good example of something that you only need to make a greasy mess out of once. Then, freeze in half-cup amounts and you can add them to soups, potatoes, salads, omelettes, etc., without a single spatter of grease.

Tip If you need chopped bacon, snip it with shears before frying it.

It's also a good idea to plan deliberate leftovers simply to vary your diet. Nobody likes eating a huge pan of enchiladas all week long, so save it in a couple of portions for another time.

But Will They Be As Good?

Yes! The key lies in wrapping your foods tightly to keep air out. If you store meals properly, they'll be scrumptious (look

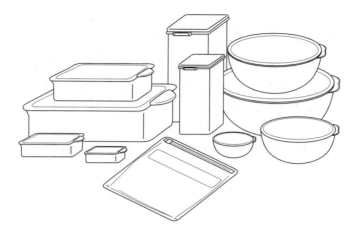

at the skyrocketing sales of frozen entrées, and you can see that just about all foods keep very nicely if wrapped correctly).

I rely heavily on rigid plastic containers with tight-fitting lids and on resealable freezer bags. If you want to wrap foods in foil or freezer paper, just be sure to fold the seams two or three times to prevent air leakage and tape securely. Keep all sealing edges clean.

Labeling is an absolute must. Even if you think you can identify something by looking at it, you will be surprised at how different food looks when it's frozen. Use masking tape and an indelible marker, and remember to label for the following:

1. What the item is

2. The amount (servings or weight)

3. The date frozen

4. Any instructions for how to use it (such as "add 2 cans broth to make soup")

(Your mom will look in your freezer and be so impressed!)

Into the Freezer

You may be wondering if all these leftovers will fit in your freezer. If you're like most cooks, you'll be pleasantly surprised at how much your freezer will really hold, especially if you stack carefully and use rectangular containers instead of round ones.

A good trick to remember is to freeze an item in its baking dish, then transfer it to a freezer bag as soon as it's frozen solid. This frees up your dish for other uses, and also makes for a perfect fit when you want to slip the frozen item back into the dish for baking or reheating.

Joni's Favorites

The best plastic wrap I have found is from Costco, an inexpensive but wonderful brand called Stretch-Tite.

I recommend freezing foods in small increments, if possible. Instead of freezing a whole roast, freeze slices. Or freeze chicken parts instead of a whole bird. This is good advice for several reasons. First, the foods will freeze faster if they're in smaller portions. They will also thaw faster if you forget to defrost ahead of time and have to fix dinner in a hurry (e.g., strips of meat for a fajita will thaw much quicker than will a whole meat loaf). And finally, they're easier to store in your freezer because you can fill in gaps with small packages and rearrange more easily.

Make sure your freezer is cold enough, or all this marvelous planning will be for nothing. Keep it set at zero degrees or lower.

Thawing

Mom may have told you this secret, but if not, listen carefully: *Do not thaw foods on the countertop.* Honestly, you are courting disaster if you put meats and entrées out at room temperature.

What happens is that the outside thaws first and gets too warm for too long (any time meat is out for more than two hours, throw it away), and bacteria goes wild. (The exception to this rule is baked goods: Most breads and cakes can be thawed on the counter for a couple of hours.)

The best way to thaw foods is in the fridge the night before or in a sinkful of cold water, which will help the outside of, say, a turkey, stay cold as the inside thaws. Other foods can be sealed in a bag to make them watertight. If you need to hurry, thaw in the microwave by using the "defrost" setting.

By the same reasoning, you also don't want to let hot foods sit on the counter "to cool" very long before freezing them. Instead, quick-chill them by plunging them into ice water (if they're wrapped well), or by placing them in the fridge to cool quickly before transferring them to the freezer. Sizzling hot food should not be placed directly into the freezer because it can alter the freezer temperature and cause everything else in there to spoil.

Tip: Place marbles in the water of your double boiler. They'll rattle and warn you when the water gets low.

Creamy foods and sauces should be reheated in the top of a double boiler; I always add a little more liquid so that they won't scorch.

Here's a good rule of thumb for cooking a casserole that's frozen solid: Cook it 1¾ hours for every quart. To keep it moist, keep it covered for the first half of its cooking time, then uncover it during the last half.

Easy Freezies

Some foods are a breeze to freeze. Here's a partial list of foods that love being frozen:

Cookie dough—Well, we may as well start with the most important one. Actually, little balls of cookie dough are one of the greatest things to freeze because the next time you need a batch of cookies (and we all know this can be a need!) you just place the frozen balls on a cookie sheet and bake them. Keep them in a resealable freezer bag and take out just what you need.

Other doughs—Bread dough, pie crust, pizza crust—they're all great to have on hand, and the freezer makes it possible.

Chopped onions and peppers—Though most vegetables have to be blanched before they can be frozen, these two can go right into the freezer in a freezer bag, to save you time later on.

Tip

Two cups of cooked ground beef equals one pound.

Overripe bananas—Freeze them right in their skins, then peel to use in smoothies, pancakes, banana bread, and milk shakes.

Miscellaneous fruits—Berries, grapes, and pineapple slices can all be placed on a cookie sheet until frozen solid, then transferred to a resealable bag.

Flour—Freezing keeps it fresh whereas storing flour at room temperature allows the grains to break down over time.

Cheesecake—Wrap tightly and it'll keep like a dream.

Pies—Fruit, pumpkin, and chiffon pies all freeze well. I recommend storing them in a waxed box. Creamy custard-type pies do not freeze as well.

Pancakes and waffles—Make a batch to freeze, then just pop one or two into the toaster when you want them.

Shredded cheese—No more moldy cheese! Just keep it in the freezer and add directly to cooked foods—because shredded cheese is so tiny, it thaws in a flash.

Butter—Freezing is a great way to take advantage of sales—stock up. Also, you'll never run out if you keep a supply in the freezer.

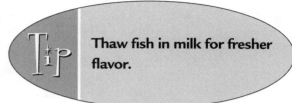

Tip

Thaw fish in milk for fresher flavor.

Nuts—Why let a stash of nuts become rancid on a pantry shelf? Nuts are expensive! Keep them frozen, just taking out as many as you need at a time.

Meats, cooked rice, cooked pastas—Just make sure they're tightly wrapped.

As you consider various recipes for freezing, keep in mind that lower-fat dishes tend to do better because fat tends to separate after it's frozen. In almost every recipe that calls for cream cheese or sour cream, you can substitute the reduced-fat version. Also look for ways to use a less-fatty substitute with milks, yogurts, oils, and cuts of meat.

And check out *The Once-a-Week Cooking Plan* (Prima Publishing, 1999) for even more information about ways to freeze various foods.

What Won't Freeze Well?

The freezing process is not a perfect match for every food. Some items wilt, turn grainy, or separate. (Look in the frozen-foods aisle for green salad—see?) Here are items you should not try to freeze:

Fresh lettuce greens

Celery

Cucumbers

Gelatin salad

Egg whites

Stuffing inside a bird

Custards

Meringue

Boiled frostings

Radishes

Whole potatoes

Eggs in the shell

Mayonnaise

How Long Will It Keep?

At least every month, you should take inventory and see what has slowly worked its way to the back of the freezer. Be sure to use foods before they get too old. Here's a guideline for several of the items you may wish to store and how long they will keep:

Soups—6 months

Butter—6 months

Soft cheese—4 months

Hard cheese—6 months

Ice cream—3 to 6 months

Pies and muffins—2 to 3 months

Breads, cakes, and cookies—6 months

Lean fish—6 months

Fatty fish—3 months

Chicken or turkey, whole—12 months

Poultry parts—9 months

Cooked chicken—1 month

Pork—3 to 6 months

Ham—2 months

Beef, lamb, and veal cuts—6 to 9 months

Ground beef—3 months

Bacon, franks, and sausage—1 month

Mashed potatoes—1 month

Cooked casseroles, soups, and stews—3 to 6 months

High-Tech Living

Let's face it. The world is computerized, satellite-ized, and push-button-ized, and there's no going back. Technology has streamlined our lives, but instead of having more leisure time, most of us are filling those extra minutes with even more achievements; more busy-ness. After all, it's a competitive world out there.

The only way to survive with your sanity intact is to make your home your haven—a place where your stress level drops and your peace quotient rises. To do this right, you need to learn the secrets of practical living so that your home is not another worry on your list, but rather a place that operates smoothly and efficiently, with an NIF (No Idiot Factor).

Freezing food plays an essential role in making life simpler—it makes sense (and cents!) to shop just once or twice a month instead of trolling the aisles every night after a hard day at work, wondering, "What should I fix tonight?" Take advantage of smart technology—and a freezer is exactly that—to make your life more organized, and thus more restful and serene.

Chapter Ten

Easy Cleanup Secrets

It's no secret that clean means healthy. We all know that our kitchen work surfaces should be as germ-free as possible, and that maintaining a clean kitchen not only looks and smells great, but prevents the spread of disease as well. So what are the easiest ways to keep a kitchen sparkling? And how can we fit all that scouring and disinfecting into our busy lives?

A Little Soak'll Do It

You will love how simple this is: Most cleaning in the kitchen can be done while you're ignoring it. Honest; much of what works best, and frees up your time the most, is letting dishes and other things soak while you accomplish something else.

Before you start cooking, your first step should be to fill a sink with hot, sudsy water. As you finish with items, toss them into the "soaking tank." By the time you've made dinner and you're ready to clean up, you can lift out most items spot-free and load them into the dishwasher. No scrubbing, no scraping.

Stove burner drip pans, burner grids, and vent hood filters can all benefit from this same soak in the sink while you're cleaning the rest of the kitchen. If you want to keep your sinks free, use a plastic dish pan.

Tip For glass pans with stubborn stains, use a quick spray of oven cleaner.

The oven is another item that can be cleaned simply by letting it set. Just place a bowl of ammonia in the oven overnight, and the next day wipe the oven clean. (This even worked for a grill rack left in a trash bag overnight.) Those ammonia fumes are powerful! If you have a self-cleaning oven, use a minivac to vacuum out the powdery, white ashes left behind; wiping down will then be a snap.

Your microwave can also be cleaning itself while you work elsewhere; place a mug or bowl of water with a slice of lemon in your microwave. Bring it to boiling, then leave the door closed as it steams for a few minutes. Spills should wipe right up.

Stubborn, burned-on food will lift right off baking pans if you sprinkle them with a bit of dishwasher soap, then let them set for a few minutes.

Stains and spills on the countertops can be sprayed with all-purpose cleaner, left alone, and then wiped right up after the chemicals have done their work.

If you're cleaning the whole house, start these soaking procedures in the kitchen first, then come back to them when everything else is done.

What's Really Dirty?

Knowing what really needs soap and scrubbing, and what doesn't, can be a big time-saver in the kitchen. If you've just rinsed lettuce in a colander, it doesn't need to go through the whole wash cycle—a simple rinse with water will make the colander clean again (this is because lettuce contains no oils, which require soap to break them down). If you've just boiled water to pour into gelatin, the water pot is still clean; indeed, it's ultraclean because you just boiled it! Sometimes we are so habituated to putting everything we touch in the dishwasher or sink when it's actually smarter to simply dry out "clean" pots and put them away.

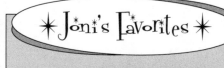

✳ Joni's Favorites ✳

I love my self-cleaning garlic press. Look for one made by Oxo, although I have friends who like the Swiss manufacturer, Susi.

Small Appliances

The key here is tiny brushes. Getting around the corners of can openers, mixers, buttons, and knobs is easiest if you have a toothbrush designated for kitchen cleaning and if you keep it handy in your under-the-sink cleaning tote, or wherever you store your all-purpose cleaner. To really get these crevices clean, spray them first with a diluted mixture of bleach and water (¼ cup bleach to a gallon of water), then scrub. The bleach will kill all bacteria.

Tip Cover oven spills with baking soda, then rub with a damp cloth.

A coffeemaker will clean up quickly if you run vinegar through a cycle, then regular water for two cycles.

Blenders clean best by blending—simply run your blender for a few seconds half filled with water and a few drops of dishwashing soap. Rinse, and it's done.

A disinfectant wet wipe is good for cleaning all kinds of surfaces, but especially those appliances that cannot be immersed or that have plug-in areas that must stay dry. Certain waffle makers, skillets, slow cookers, and countless other electrical gadgets must be wiped clean, not washed in water.

Cabinets

A handheld minivac is a great tool for eliminating powders and crumbs that accumulate in the pantry or in cupboards where you store cereals, cocoa, cake mixes, and such. If pests are a problem, place dry goods in resealable plastic bags (such as Ziploc) or in sturdy plastic containers with tight-fitting lids (such as Tupperware). You'll contain every last grain of salt!

To thoroughly clean cabinets, remove everything from a shelf, then wipe down with a disinfectant. Let the shelf dry, then wipe the bottoms of your packages and return them to the shelf. Wipe clean any jar lids with sticky spills. Extra lids and stray Tupperware tops make good coasters to keep under jars that tend to get sticky.

Tip *A computer mouse pad will loosen jar lids.*

How old are your drawer and cabinet liners? If they're torn or stained, it's time to replace them. Plain paper works, but consider all options before you buy; you might want to invest in something rubberized to reduce breakage or noise, or a thicker liner that will last longer.

Once cabinets are wiped down, run a cleaning cloth around the tops and sides of the cabinet door (door tops are infamous dust catchers). Now clean the inside surface of the door, then the outside, looking especially for stubborn fingerprints.

Counters and Cutting Boards

These need constant attention, as they're the surfaces on which we place our food and work with it. I keep a package of disinfecting wipes in a handy drawer and use them often. A spritzer of diluted bleach or all-purpose cleaner and a roll of paper towels also work well.

Do not just grab the sponge from the sink and wipe it over spills or crumbs. You'll be spreading bacteria and making matters worse, as sponges are notorious breeding grounds. (If you microwave a wet sponge for a minute or so, you can disinfect it. I also run sponges through the dishwasher daily.) But if you want really clean counters, you need to use really clean towels on it. This is probably why I go through so many paper towels; I like the idea of using them once and throwing them away.

Tip

To sanitize kitchen counters quickly, keep a small spray bottle of diluted bleach under the sink.

And don't forget to clean the back splash, the wall just behind your counters. It gets dirty, too.

Cutting boards are one of the riskiest channels in the kitchen for spreading illness. I recommend having two boards, one for meats and one for vegetables, so you won't risk getting raw chicken drippings on your tomatoes. After every use, spray with diluted bleach and let dry completely.

Eating Areas

Whether it's a breakfast bar or a dining table, these popular spots tend to clutter up with school backpacks, mail, projects, and what have you. Once a surface is cluttered, it's ten times harder to clean. So how do you keep it uncluttered?

Keep cloth placemats cleaner by spraying them with Scotch Guard when you first bring them home.

You set the table and keep it set all day. That's it—you put out the dishes, the glasses, everything you need for dinner that night. Now there's nowhere to dump a stack of library books or a pile of work supplies. Your family will just have to find somewhere else to put their stuff (the proper place, let us hope).

And you know what? Your table now looks like a picture in a magazine! It's decorated, it's inviting (but only for eating), and it will even save you time when it's actually time to eat. I know a woman who sets her dinner table every morning when she unloads dishes from the dishwasher. It looks gorgeous all day, like something out of a model home.

Babies and toddlers can destroy good tablecloths. If you want the look of lovely linen but you also have some messy eaters, cover it with a thick sheet of clear vinyl from a fabric store—spills will wipe right up.

Dish Duty

If you have kids, make a chore chart and let them share in the cleanup duties (cooking, too, if they're old enough). Use a dishpan or a rolling tea cart to gather the dirty dishes and save trips to the kitchen. Teach them that they're not through with the dishes until the table, stove, and counters have been wiped down as well.

Hand wash crystal and valuable china over a rubber mat in the sink (or at least over a dish towel) to minimize the chances of chipping or breakage. Sharp knives should also be hand washed to keep them from dulling and to prevent accidents when they're being reached for in a dishwasher.

Tip

Keep a steel scouring pad in a clay saucer to prevent it from rusting—the saucer will absorb moisture and keep the pad dry.

Faucets and chrome will shine right up if you wipe them with rubbing alcohol. A used fabric-softener sheet from the dryer is another good shiner. To prevent water spots, spritz faucets with a fast spray of nonstick cooking oil, then wipe them off.

Teach your family to clean up as they go, and your work will be cut in half. Kids often need reminding to wash their hands when they come home from school or in from play—not only will this prevent the spread of germs, but the surfaces they touch will stay cleaner looking, too.

The Refrigerator

Doesn't it feel great when you stock a new refrigerator? Everything is gleaming and bright; even the food looks better. You can keep your fridge looking clean and new by preventing messes in the first place (then I'll tell you how to clean up if it's too late!).

Line crispers with paper towels. These not only keep the crispers cleaner, they also absorb the excess moisture that ruins our vegetables.

Use ice-cube bins to corral like items. I have one that contains nothing but mustards, another that contains jams and jellies, another for pickles and relishes. Any jars that drip will drip into the bin, not through all the grates and shelves of my fridge. Also, it's easier to assemble sandwiches or whatever if you can just lift out one container that holds all your condiments. Think of them as food files!

> **Tip**
> Use a spatula instead of a knife when spreading mayonnaise on sandwiches—it's much faster.

Throw away questionable foods. Each day you reach into the refrigerator for something fresh, see if you can also take out something that's getting too old to be in there. Not only will this free up space and keep your fridge from overcrowding, your fridge will smell better, too.

> **Tip**
> Keep an open box of baking soda in the back of the fridge to absorb odors.

When it's time for a thorough cleaning, remove everything from the fridge. Don't worry about spoilage; this isn't going to take all afternoon. Baking soda mixed with water is generally a good refrigerator cleaner and a remover of unpleasant odors, but often you'll need to use all-purpose cleaners to attack hard or sticky spills. Remove bins and crispers and wash them in hot soapy water. Use the back side of a hard plastic pancake turner to scrape spills off plastic surfaces.

And don't forget to clean the gaskets, those rubber seals around the doors; they somehow collect a myriad of crumbs and dirt.

Last, wipe off jars and bottles before you put them back in the fridge. Spray the outside door and wipe off fingerprints, and be sure to dust on top and underneath your fridge. Now you're all done.

Floors

This is the final cleaning frontier, no matter which room you are cleaning. Floors are always last, as that's where the dust and dirt will settle as you clean other areas.

I always vacuum my kitchen floor before I mop it, just to remove as much dirt as possible. Then I get two buckets ready and a good wet mop. One bucket holds my diluted Murphy's Soap, as I have wood floors, and the other is for dirty-mop rinses. You can use the same procedure on linoleum or tile; just be sure to use the appropriate cleaner for the kind of floor you have.

Wrap a rag (or old pantyhose) around the end of a broom handle or yardstick for reaching under ovens and other tricky spaces. Don't forget to check baseboards, especially if yours have molding or edges that could collect dust and grease.

Launder any rugs and replace them after you've cleaned the floor. Now sit down and enjoy a tall, frosty glass of lemonade in your beautiful, clean kitchen. For more information on keeping your entire house clean and inviting, see *Housekeeping Secrets My Mother Never Taught Me* (Prima Publishing, 2001).

Chapter Eleven

Other Tricks
Good Cooks Know

When you've cooked for several years, you accumulate a storehouse of shortcuts and tricks that make cooking easier and better. You've made mistakes, and you've learned which ones don't make any difference. You've also mastered the techniques that produce consistently delicious food. Most cooks share this wisdom while they're cooking, like an oral history, passed from parent to child. The problem is, few families actually cook together anymore, and thus many wonderful traditions and secrets are getting lost. Here are some hints your mother may not have told you (or Grandma may not have told her!).

Be Prepared

Read the whole recipe before you start—what if something has to chill for several hours? Also, when you ask a friend for a recipe, sometimes it isn't written cookbook style, with all the ingredients listed in the order you'll use them. You may run across stray ingredients in the instructions (top with whipped cream, serve over rice, garnish with grated cheese, etc.), and reading it through first will ensure that you have everything on hand.

Keep a well-stocked pantry of non-perishables that you can work from if company suddenly surprises you. The following is a good, comprehensive list:

Flour	Shortening
Sugar (granulated, brown, powdered)	Spices
Salt	Cocoa powder
Pepper	Cereals
Oil	Ketchup and other condiments
Vinegar	Mayonnaise
Spices and extracts	Salad dressings
Cornstarch	Soy sauce
Yeast (if you bake bread)	Worcestershire sauce
Corn syrup	Pasta
Maple syrup	Pasta sauce
Canned milk	Tomato paste
Buttermilk baking mix	Tomato sauce
Nuts	Applesauce
Baking soda	Canned broth

Canned meats, such as tuna

Canned vegetables/fruits

Canned soups

Chocolate chips

Baking chocolate

Oatmeal

Rice

Peanut butter

Jam

Fruit juices

Whole garlic

Onions

Potatoes

Crackers

Mixes for cakes, soups, muffins, etc.

Of course there will be a number of items that you'll want to have in the refrigerator, such as the following:

Milk

Butter

Cream

Cream cheese

Sour cream

Hard cheeses

Yogurt

Opened condiment jars, which must be refrigerated after opening

Lettuce

Celery

Produce that should be kept chilled

Juice

Eggs

Cooked meats

Lunch meat

Salsa

Mayonnaise (Once opened mayonnaise must be chilled.)

Dips

Leftovers that are to be eaten promptly

Chocolate milk, just because

It's also a good idea to keep certain components of your favorite recipes in the freezer, such as the following:

Cooked ground beef with chopped onions (no skillet to wash when you thaw it out!)

Cooked shredded chicken

Cooked pasta, drained

Shredded cheese

Balls of cookie dough

Frozen berries

Soup components (you just add the broth)

Baked bread loaves, muffins

Frozen bread dough

Beef patties

Pie crusts

Pizza crusts

Blanched fruits and veggies

Cakes (just thaw and frost)

Cooked rice

Assembling recipes becomes a snap when the most time-consuming steps are already done.

Baking Tips

Make sure your ingredients are at room temperature—you don't want to try to soften the butter in the microwave and end up with some stiff parts and some liquified parts. Put things out long before you're ready to use them so they can be easily combined. Eggs should be at room temperature also, but if you're in the middle of a recipe and just now remembered the eggs, run them under warm water to take the chill off. Pie dough, of course, is the exception to this rule, as it requires ice water to mix up properly.

If you're rolling out biscuits and don't have a round biscuit cutter, use the rim of a drinking glass. Dip it in flour first so it won't stick.

When any recipe calls for brown sugar, it means *packed* brown sugar. Use the bottom of a glass to press it down in a measuring cup so you'll get a flat top to compare to the measurement lines.

When a recipe calls for 2 cups whipping cream, it means the pourable, *un*whipped cream. If it says 2 cups *whipped* cream, then the cream must be whipped first and then measured.

To decorate cakes and pastries, keep a shaker of powdered sugar handy; it saves time instead of using a sifter. A separate shaker for flour makes it easy to dust baking pans or flour a work surface.

When recipes call for separated eggs, just use your clean hands. Let the whites slide through your fingers as the yolk remains in your palm. Some cooks pour the egg back and forth from one half of the shell to the other, but this risks breaking the yolk on the sharp edge of the shell.

Don't try to use sweetened condensed milk (which is very sweet) in place of evaporated milk (which is simply milk with 60 percent of the water removed). Read the recipe carefully and be sure you're using the right one. To save money and space, consider using powdered milk (nonfat dry milk) in baked goods.

Most people overcook chocolate when trying to melt it. Place the chips or chunks you wish to melt in a heat-proof glass cup or bowl and microwave them, just thirty seconds at a time. Take them out when they've heated but still appear to be chips; stir and watch as they melt from the existing heat already in them. Your chocolate should stay glossy and smooth this way. Never let water get into the chocolate mixture; if you need to soften it a little, add a bit of shortening or paraffin wax. You can also melt chocolate in the top of a double boiler, but again, don't let it overcook.

If your fudge is crumbly, you need to adjust the ratio of fats and sugars—increase the fat and decrease the sugar.

Beginning cooks tend to overbake pecan pie, pumpkin pie, puddings and curds, forgetting that they will thicken upon cooling.

When preparing most recipes for baking, first mix the wet ingredients together, then add the dry ones. You'll have a better batter!

✳ Joni's Favorites ✳

Try to find a tapered rolling pin. The renowned pastry chef, Ettore, taught me the following: If the rolling pin is thicker in the middle and smaller at the ends, you can roll dough more uniformly, as you eliminate the problem of thin outer edges. And you don't need handles— just roll on the wood.

If you hear of a great recipe you'd like to try but don't know what temperature to use, try 350 degrees—it's the most common oven setting—then periodically check the food.

If a recipe doesn't say whether to place cookies on a greased or ungreased baking sheet, take no chances—use parchment paper (it makes cleanup easier, too).

Instead of greasing pans with shortening, try a spray of nonstick oil.

To make a perfect tart crust, push a rolling pin over the tart pan. This effectively cuts off the crust at the exact level of the fluted edge of the pan.

Before filling a pastry bag, fold it down halfway. It will then stay cleaner when you fold it up.

Joni's Favorites

I always keep bouillon granules on hand. They add richness and depth to many soups and sauces.

Whipped cream will hold its shape if you mix a teaspoon of unflavored gelatin into each cup of cream you beat.

For the tallest, fluffiest cakes, use cake flour instead of regular flour.

For special occasions, substitute whole cream for the milk in pancakes. Or, throw in a handful of chocolate chips for a real treat.

Add vanilla and cinnamon to your French toast egg mixture for extra flavor. If it's holiday time, substitute eggnog for the milk.

To cut down on the fat in baked goods, substitute applesauce or another fruit puree for half the oil.

Bread that didn't rise can still be brushed with olive oil, garlic, and Parmesan, and passed off as a new kind of focaccia bread!

Specific Products

Meats look better browned than pale (so brown them first), but sometimes you can doctor up a pale appearance with Kitchen Bouquet. This product has been around for years, and just a few drops will turn pale gravy brown.

Lumpy gravy can be avoided if you first shake the flour with water in a lidded jar. Then pour it into the drippings and stir. Another great product for ensuring lump-free sauces and gravies is Wondra, a flour made by Gold Medal.

Fruits that brown quickly when sliced, such as apples and bananas, will stay fresh looking with a sprinkling of Fruit Fresh or a brush of lemon juice.

Chicken can be coated with almost any seasoning packet, then baked. Even packets intended for beef, such as Swedish meatball mix or taco mix, will work.

For an outdoor barbecue taste for your meats and sauces, Liquid Smoke is the product. Even a small amount will do it.

✳ Joni's Favorites ✳

I found a sugar and spice blend so spectacular I have to recommend it—it's great for cinnamon toast, yams, cooked apples, ice cream, snickerdoodles, and many more desserts. It's called Vanilla Cinnamon Sugar and it's made by Charles Baldwin and Sons Chemists in West Stockbridge, Massachusetts.
To order, call (413) 232-7785 or check their Web site at www.baldwinextracts.com on the Internet.

Using Your Microwave

Most people use their microwaves just for reheating leftovers and making popcorn. But it can do so much more and save you hours of time. Here are some easy ways to make microwave cooking part of your lifestyle:

Warm seedless jams in the microwave to use as glazes.

Warm up syrup for pancakes.

Soften ice cream for scooping—30 seconds should do it.

Soften butter by zapping for a few seconds at a time.

Soften tightly wrapped brown sugar.

Thaw frozen juice (remove metal lid first).

Melt chocolate chips.

Thaw cream cheese, whipped toppings.

Defrost ground beef and other meats; use the 30 percent setting.

Dry slices of bread for making bread crumbs.

Warm up citrus so it will yield more juice.

Crisp up stale cereals and crackers.

Bake quick breads and brownies in microwave-safe dishes.

Partially cook food in the microwave, then finish on the barbecue grill for great grilled flavor.

Toast nuts or coconut.

Scramble eggs and cook them in a small bowl for a fat-free meal.

Make s'mores by melting chocolate chips and mini-marshmallows between graham crackers.

Tip

Give cake mixes home-made flavor by adding ½ teaspoon butter-flavored extract and ½ teaspoon vanilla extract.

Create greaseless quesadillas—heat cheese and chilies between two flour tortillas until cheese begins to melt.

Soften a slice of cake until the frosting is gooey.

Heat up oatmeal and other breakfast cereals.

Cook bacon on a rack that drains it, or on paper towels.

Zap corn on the cob for eight minutes.

Roast a chicken in one-quarter the time it usually takes.

Make tuna melts, ham melts, turkey melts.

Bake casseroles.

Boil water in your glass measuring cup.

If unsure about a cooking time, halve it and check the food before finishing cooking.

Cover meats and other dishes that could splatter with an inverted paper plate.

Place denser pieces of meat on the outside, smaller pieces on the inside, for even cooking.

Once meat has browned in your regular oven, let it finish cooking (faster) in the microwave.

Use the four-to-one formula—it will take four times as long to cook the same thing in a conventional oven.

Use round dishes for uniform cooking.

Shape foods into a ring so you won't have an uncooked center.

Remember that foods continue to cook even after the microwave finishes.

Cooking Tips

To make perfect hard-cooked eggs, do not boil them. Place cold eggs in cold water that is at least an inch deeper than the eggs. (If an egg floats, it's old—throw it out.) Place the saucepan on a cold burner, then turn on the heat and let the water come to a full boil. Cover the eggs, remove them from the heat, and let them sit for fifteen minutes. Rinse with cool water to prevent further cooking. This will keep the yolks yellow, instead of oxidizing into the familiar gray-green we've all seen. To peel eggs, roll them on the counter to crack the shell, then peel under running water.

Tip
Hard-cooked eggs won't crack if you add a little salt to the water.

Keep rice in your salt shaker to prevent salt from getting lumpy.

A bay leaf in your dry-goods pantry will repel bugs.

Keep brown sugar soft by wrapping it tightly or storing it with an apple.

Ripen fruit by placing it in a paper bag for a day or two; the gases released will hasten its ripening.

Before you bake carrots (around a roast, for example), parboil them—carrots are so woody that they need a little extra help. It's also a good idea to parboil ribs and sausage to remove much of the grease before baking or frying them.

Tip
Plastic containers won't stain with tomato sauce if you coat them with nonstick spray before filling them.

It's easy to peel a tomato when making fresh tomato sauce if you first blanch it. Simply immerse the tomato in boiling water for thirty seconds and the skin should slip off easily.

When making jelly, add a dab of butter to each jar to cut the foam.

Cook rice, pasta, and polenta in flavored water—use chicken stock, vegetable stock, a broth, or a juice.

Roasted garlic cloves are much milder, and easier to digest, than raw ones. You can use more of them—sprinkle around a roasted cut of meat. (Cloves of raw garlic will flavor steaks and cook beautifully if you tuck them into the meat itself before cooking.)

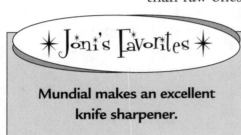

Joni's Favorites

Mundial makes an excellent knife sharpener.

If you need to pound a cutlet to make it thinner, place it between two pieces of waxed paper and pound it with the bottom of a saucepan (this takes less time than using a mallet).

If preparing shish kebab on bamboo skewers, be sure to soak the skewers in water for twenty minutes first to prevent scorching.

Scrambled eggs will cook up fluffier if you mix in a bit of water instead of milk.

Use a light touch when salting cheese dishes—cheese is already quite salty.

Many Asian cooks use only a cleaver for all cutting purposes. When using one, inch your hand up close to the blade and place your thumb on the dull edge of the metal for extra support. When chopping or mincing with a chef's knife, press down on the tip with your free hand and rock the knife back and forth to cut the food.

Stale crackers and chips can be freshened if you flash them under cold water and then bake in the oven for a few minutes to crisp them up again.

When reheating a soup, stew, or pasta, add a little extra water to keep it from sticking to the bottom of the pan; it won't affect the recipe, as the water will steam off.

Clarified butter is easy to make and keeps well in the refrigerator. Melt butter and discard the clouded part, pouring the clear part into a jar. Use it for sautéing, as it will not burn as quickly as regular butter will.

Don't allow your kids to roll corn cobs in the butter, and don't fight with dabs that keep slipping off the knife. Simply melt the butter in the microwave and brush it over all the cobs before serving them.

If mashed potatoes seem like too much work, make life easier: Don't peel the potatoes. Wash, quarter, and boil them. Drain, then use an electric mixer to mash them. Add a bit of milk, butter, sour cream, salt, and pepper—delicious.

Fresh pineapple is easy to prepare and it always delights everyone. Begin with a pineapple that smells fragrant and that

has loose top leaves. Chop off both ends, then set it up and slice thinly down the sides, removing the skin. If the eyes are deep, cut diagonal Vs in the pineapple to follow the row of eyes and remove them. Now slice vertically again, close to the core to remove long spears of juicy pineapple. Serve whole spears or cut them into cross sections.

To slice apples for pies, cut off both ends, then peel. Now slice in half and remove core with a melon baller. The apple halves are now ready to be thinly sliced into uniform pieces.

Get to know your butcher and ask him or her to show you how to bone a chicken (you'll save a fortune), how to cut meats across the grain, and so forth. Free cooking lessons!

If you want to cut the fat in baked chicken, bake it with the skin on (for flavor), *then* remove the skin.

When stirring cheese into a soup, make sure the soup is not boiling hot. Cheese will turn lumpy if it's too hot—just swirl it slowly into a warm/hot soup.

Soup and hot drinks will cool faster if you rest a spoon in them (the metal handle will conduct heat away). And never drink a hot cider or broth with a straw; you can get a severe burn.

The best way to peel an orange is to score the skin in four vertical cuts, like longitude lines. Each section should then peel in one easy strip.

Chapter Twelve

Basic Food Repair

everybody's had cooking disasters. Rolls burn, ovens short out, salads wilt and sauces curdle. Sometimes you just have to throw out the whole mess and call for pizza. And often the mishap is out of your control, like the hungry family members who eat the raspberries you were saving. When I was 15, I nibbled on my mom's roast chicken as I talked on the phone to my best friend, and an hour later there was nothing left but the carcass. Sorry, Mom. Teenagers happen, too.

But sometimes, if you're clever, you can find the chocolate lining, and still use foods that didn't turn out quite right. Or, if you know the tricks, you can prevent problems in the first place. Here are some ways to salvage items that look hopeless, or to solve common kitchen dilemmas.

Minor Miracles

Honey that has turned to sugar: Heat on stove top or in microwave; it will liquify again.

Gelatin that didn't set: Freeze it. Or, beat it with a stiff dairy product such as cream cheese or whipped cream and chill again. Or, since you probably added too much liquid, heat the mixture again to boiling and stir in another packet of gelatin.

Undercooked corn on the cob: Reboil, or use a paring knife to remove kernels and toss with a green salad. (You can also cut the kernels off with a clean metal shoe horn.)

Joni's Favorites

I think Cuisinart makes the best food processor.

Too much silk on corn cobs: Rub it off with a dampened paper towel.

Overripe bananas: Mash and freeze them in an ice-cube tray. When frozen solid, pop them out and store them in a freezer bag to use for fruit smoothies, pancakes, muffins, and banana bread.

Dry bread slices: Whirl in blender or food processor and save as bread crumbs. Or make bread pudding, or stuffing.

Fudge or jam that didn't thicken: Use as ice-cream toppings or pancake syrup.

Apples no longer crisp: Peel, dice, and sauté with sugar and cinnamon to make applesauce. Or, chop and make into apple cake.

Watery mashed potatoes: Use as a thickener for soups or sauces (they may be frozen for this later use).

Ice cream nobody will eat: Mix with equal parts self-rising flour, throw in some nuts and raisins, and bake as muffin dough.

Gummy rice: Mix with grated cheddar cheese and an egg, then fry as patties. Or, stir into meat loaf. Or, sauté with oil and soy sauce to make fried rice, cooking off the excess moisture. Or, make a rice crust for a spinach quiche. (Next time add a squeeze of lemon as you boil the rice; it will keep the grains separate.)

Peanut butter and syrups stick to measuring cup: First spray the cup with nonstick oil. This works on measuring spoons, too.

Wilted celery: Cut off stem ends and place in refrigerated pitcher of water; they'll soon be crisp again.

Wilted vegetables: Cut off brown edges, rinse with water, wrap in a paper towel, and chill for an hour.

Whipped cream won't whip: Chill cream, bowl, and beaters, then try again. Or, add a few drops of lemon juice.

Whipped cream is watery: Add an egg white, chill, then beat again. (Prevent this problem by adding a teaspoon of gelatin to each cup of cream when you whip it.)

Batters and flour coatings fall off chicken: Pat chicken dry with paper towels before coating. Then chill for an hour in the fridge so coating can "set."

Dried-out mushrooms: Whirl in processor or blender, mix with water, and freeze in ice-cube trays—pop one out and add it to soups, casseroles, scrambled eggs, sauces.

Poached eggs spread too much: Add a dash of vinegar to the cooking water.

Pies bubble over onto oven: Place a baking sheet on the lowest rack to catch the spills.

Baked potatoes too hard: Microwave for one-fourth the time you still need in the oven. (In the future, boil potatoes in salted water for 10 minutes before baking them; they'll bake faster.)

Overcooked meat: Mince and mix with quiche ingredients for a savory main-dish pie.

> **Tip**
> Sticky raisins will break apart easily if you freeze them.

Leftover veggies from a vegetable party platter: Stir-fry with garlic, ginger, and soy sauce.

Leftover meat: Make a pita fajita. Sauté sliced onion and peppers in a dash of oil. Add some salsa and sliced meat, until just heated through. Spoon into pita bread pockets.

Leftover scrambled eggs: Chop and mix with spinach in a salad with vinaigrette dressing. Chop and mix with fried rice. Chop and mix with mayonnaise for a sandwich filling.

Leftover baked potatoes: Rinse with water, then rebake at 350 degrees for 20 minutes.

Butter burns in frying pan: Mix butter with equal parts oil to prevent burning. Also, heat the pan before you add the butter.

Water boils over: Add a spoonful of butter or oil.

Oil spatters when frying: Add salt.

Brown sugar is hard: Microwave to soften. Or, grate. Or, store with a slice of soft bread to soften in two hours. Store with an apple slice to prevent future hardening.

Hard raisins: Soak in warm water to plump, then mix them into cookie dough or cinnamon rolls.

Overcooked, limp vegetables: Whirl in blender or processor to made a delicious vegetable stock, the basis for many soups and sauces.

Overcooked bread: Cube, dip in garlic butter, then bake until crispy for salad croutons.

Stale bread: Flash under cold water, then bake at 400 degrees for a few minutes to crisp the crust again.

Cookies no one will eat: Dip in melted chocolate, then crushed nuts. Or, crush them to use as a crunchy ice-cream topping. Or, grind them finely and use them to make pie crust.

Broken crackers: Crush until crumbs. Rub chicken with mayonnaise, then coat with cracker crumbs. Bake for 1 hour at 350 degrees. Or, use in meat loaf, salmon patties, or as a casserole topping.

Overcooked franks: Chop, then use like crumbled bacon: Mix with scrambled eggs, or with baked beans.

Meat loaf that falls apart: Mix it with spaghetti sauce and cooked pasta. Or, bake it into a casserole with veggies and cheese. Or, make it into chili.

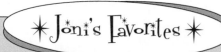

✳ Joni's Favorites ✳

I have a Heavy Duty KitchenAid and it is fabulous. But just as often I grab my little handheld mixer and take it to the stove to whip potatoes, or to another counter to whip cream. If I had to choose only one, I'd probably pick the portable.

Meat loaf that sticks to pan: Place it on a small grid/rack, or place a slice of bacon underneath before cooking.

Ketchup won't pour: Insert a drinking straw or knife, then remove it. Or, tap on the side of the bottle, rather than the bottom.

Kitchen fills with smoke when broiling: Fill bottom of broiler with water to absorb smoke.

Fruit too soft to eat: Whirl into a fruit smoothie. Or mash it and freeze it in paper cups for fruit pops.

Cake that crumbles: Break up cake and layer the crumbles with pudding and fruit in a trifle bowl. Or, press an inch of cake chunks into the bottom of a loaf pan, cover with an inch of ice cream, and repeat layers two more times to make an ice cream torte.

Soggy pizza crust: Place on skillet and "fry" in a bit of oil until moisture evaporates.

Biscuits that fall apart: Serve with gravy. Or, stir into a chicken-pot-pie mixture.

Stale cinnamon rolls: Tear up and make into bread pudding.

Too-salty soup: Add a dash of sugar and vinegar, or cook it with a cut potato, which will absorb much of the salt, then discard the potato.

Too-spicy foods: Add sour cream or another dairy product to cut the intensity of the spice. A sweetener such as sugar or honey may also help.

Pasta too hard: Reboil.

Lumpy or curdled sauce: Pour through strainer and discard lumps.

Drippings too greasy: Chill or freeze and remove solidified top layer of fat. Swirl an ice cube through greasy soup to do the same thing.

Edges of flour tortillas dried out: Cut off and discard dry portion. Cut remaining tortillas into three-inch strips and use as noodles for lasagna.

Peanut butter coated with layer of oil: Stir thoroughly.

Stale french bread: Slice lengthwise, cover with pizza sauce and mozzarella, broil to make pizzas.

Top pie crust burned: Discard top crust, warm the rest, and serve it with ice cream as a cobbler.

Fallen cakes: Frost anyway and cut as brownies.

Burned anything: Call it Cajun blackened!

Hard avocados: Mash into guacamole.

Too many "old maids" in popcorn: Next time, freeze the kernels, or rinse them with ice water, before you pop them.

Cake too dry: Serve with a sauce such as vanilla sauce, raspberry sauce, or lemon curd.

Too much of one ingredient added to batter: Double the batch.

Casserole looks unattractive: Cover with grated cheese or a mixture of bread crumbs, Parmesan, and melted butter.

Dough for cut-out cookies keeps tearing: Chill completely, then roll out thicker.

Cake won't come out of pan: Run knife around edge, set pan on wet towel, or reheat cake for five minutes.

Soup or sauce too thin: Add instant potato flakes.

Soup too greasy: Stir a lettuce leaf into the soup; oil will adhere to it, then you can remove it.

Gravy too thin: Add a thin paste of cornstarch and water, heat gravy until thickened.

Gravy too greasy: Add a pinch of baking soda.

Main dish too sweet: Add a dash of cayenne pepper or another hot spice to counteract the sweetness. Or, stir in a bit of vinegar.

Seafood cakes fall apart: Mix with a white sauce and serve over toasted English muffins.

Sweet sauce too grainy: Reheat until sugar granules dissolve.

Candy too sticky: Store in an uncovered container. Or (if it won't melt) bake briefly—five minutes, then check it—in a cool oven, 200 degrees.

Frosting too stiff: Add canned milk and stir again.

Citrus too dry: Microwave to get more juice flowing. Grate peel to use as seasoning.

Cake frosting sticks to plastic wrap: Spray the plastic with a thin film of nonstick cooking spray before placing it over the cake.

Cheese drying out: Grate and stir into hot soup. (Prevent this next time by coating the edge with butter or wrapping the cheese in a cloth dampened with vinegar.)

Top of cheesecake cracked: Cover with a fruit topping.

Chocolate "blooming" (getting chalky white spots): This will not affect its flavor. Melt or use anyway.

Cabbage smells strong: Add a little vinegar to the cooking water.

Yams too soft: Beat with mixer, adding brown sugar and melted butter; spread in a buttered baking dish and bake at 350 degrees for 15 minutes.

Food too blah: Salt is not the only way to bring out flavor. Try a dash of mustard, lime juice, curry, chopped chilies, or Tabasco sauce.

Rubbery meringue (this often happens with leftover pie): Pull off meringue and top with whipped cream instead.

Weeping meringue: Add a teaspoon of cornstarch to the sugar before beating it into the eggs.

Pancakes raw inside: Slice in half horizontally and cook again (next time make them thinner, or reduce the frying temperature).

And if your food disaster is actually a food that has soured or gotten fuzzy, don't try to remake it into anything—just toss it out.

Part Four

Beyond
Basic

Chapter Thirteen

Entertaining

*

My kids inform me that 76 percent of all statistics are made up, so here's another one: Half of all the people who entertain are miserable doing it.

You want to be in the other half. And I'm going to show you how to do it. First, let's look at how to eliminate such anxiety when it comes to throwing a party.

Planning Ahead

The secret here is organization. If you try to throw a lavish feast at the last minute, you're going to be panicked—there will be too many expectations for something elaborate and you'll feel pressured to rise to the occasion with handmade place cards and a ten-course meal. The house won't be as clean as you'd like, and halfway through the party you'll remember the appetizers and the frozen butter carving you forgot to put out. You'll be so busy stressing and cooking that you won't even have time to socialize. You'll sink into bed that night exhausted and vowing never to entertain again. This is the result of poor planning.

A successful party begins with pencil and paper. Choose a date that falls on the day after your regular cleaning day so that you'll be rested and your house will be tidy. Is your party in honor of a special event? What's in bloom at that moment that will make for a pretty centerpiece? What fruits are in season? Will you be in the throes of PMS? Is it the same night as the playoffs? It's important to pick a date that works well for you, as well as for your guests. Be flexible if some of the key invitees have other plans; have a backup date to offer them.

Write down whom you wish to invite. Now plan backward. Two weeks before the date, send out the invitations or call the guests. Two weeks gives people ample time to plan, but not so much time that they forget about your event. If you're having a big group, you don't need RSVPs; just plan food for forty, or for however many you're inviting. (Party thrower's secret: RSVPs are horribly unreliable; people say they can come and don't, while others say they can't and then suddenly show up. And this is if you hear from them at all.) But, if you're having a small gathering of six or eight people, you need to determine if each guest can make it and then plug holes with B-list people if they can't so you won't have conspicuously empty chairs around your table.

Plan your menu. I've provided some great ideas below to make this easier. When choosing recipes, include plenty of things that can be prepared in advance so you don't greet your guests in a panting sweat, with a timer going off in the background.

Plan what you're going to wear—make sure it's back from the cleaners if necessary—and allow yourself time to bathe, do your hair, and get ready. Many hostesses set their table the night before so that there's one less thing to worry about.

Here's a twenty-point checklist to help you plan the rest of the details:

1. If it's a sit-down dinner, where will you seat each person? Have you combined personalities that will harmonize? Sit boy-girl-boy-girl if possible, and try to separate people who already know each other and might spend the whole evening in a private buzz session rather than mingling with the other guests.

2. Is somebody going to give a toast or make an announcement? Arrange for this if necessary.

3. What kind of music will be playing in the background? (Secret: Keep it low if this is an intimate gathering where everyone at the dining table is in the same conversation; keep it louder if it's a cocktail party and you don't want an awkward silence to fill the room.) Choose music that will likely appeal to a large group.

4. Will there be any parking or noisy-band problems, and, if so, have you alerted your neighbors?

5. Are you going to have any kind of decorations, on the table or elsewhere? Is your centerpiece low enough that people can see each other over it? Are you making the centerpiece yourself, and, if so, have you allowed enough time for this?

6. Are you giving each person a party favor?

7. Do you need place cards?

8. Do you have room in the coat closet for guests' wraps?

9. If it's a buffet, where will you place the chairs for sitting and eating, and how will traffic flow around the buffet table? Do you need to borrow or rent extra chairs?

10. What plates and utensils will you be using and will you have enough?

11. Is it clear how to enter your home? Many houses get more traffic through a side door than the front. Make it clear where you want guests to arrive, and keep the walkway swept and unobstructed.

12. Does the front door/porch look inviting? Do you need to freshen a wreath or shake out a mat?

13. Is your tablecloth (if you're using one) ironed?

14. Do you have the refrigerator/freezer space for the food you're planning, and, if not, do you have ice chests? (If this is a Christmas-caroling party, and you live where it's cold, use your back porch as extra fridge space!)

15. If it's an outdoor party, do you have a contingency plan if it should rain?

16. Is anybody allergic to something, or on a special diet? (Really, it's their obligation to let you know, but humans are human and they forget. So ask.)

17. Do your plans fit your budget? Price out what you'll have to buy and see if you need to cut back. You don't want to be the father of the bride who can't enjoy the reception because he's agonizing over the price tag.

18. Have you prepared these dishes before, or are they new recipes? If new, try them out first.

19. Have you considered any other parties or gatherings you need to have? As long as the house is immaculate and the flowers are fresh, why not throw two parties back-to-back and have a second group over?

20. Is the guest bath sparkling clean, with fresh soap and towels available?

> Tip
>
> Keep pests at bay when eating on the patio—place a vase of fresh marigolds on the table.

Believe me, your stress level will drop immensely if you have all of these details ironed out in advance.

Greetings

When guests arrive, welcome them with enthusiasm, even if the hors d'oeuvres just scorched in the kitchen. Remember, parties are about people, not the details that tend to sidetrack us.

Never apologize for your home. This is your domain, and you have invited loved ones to come into these intimate quarters and break bread with you. It is an honor for you that they came, and they in turn should be honored that they were invited. Whether you're remodeling, didn't have time to prune the trees out front, or haven't re-covered the sofa yet, say nothing about that. Focus on your guests and making sure they feel welcome. Besides, if you don't draw attention to a problem, your guests probably won't notice it.

Offer to take their coats and hang them up, if at all possible. Throwing them over a bed is all right if you've run out of closet space, but jackets wrinkle and things fall out of pockets this way. Hanging them is really best.

Always offer guests something to drink, even if it's just ice water. And give them a napkin with it.

Take time when guests arrive to introduce them to at least one other person; this allows them to begin a conversation and thus avoid standing in the middle of a room like a lone ice cube floating in a punch bowl.

If people are strangers to each other, or relatively shy, plan a way to help them get acquainted—give them a mystery to solve or a guessing game to play, or provide some clues about each other or areas of common ground.

If serving drinks or appetizers, plan to eat about 45 minutes after arrival time. If not, seat everyone within half an hour, or when there's a lull in conversation and you can let guests start on salad.

Rules of etiquette say you should never discuss religion or politics, but people do it anyway. Keep tabs on your guests out of the corner of your eye, and if a conversation gets too heated, be prepared to intervene with a fascinating change of subject and/or to pull one guest away if necessary: "Did you know there's always a meteor shower in the middle of August? Let's go outside and see if we can see some shooting stars." "Did you see Kim's new watch—it gives surfing conditions on it!" "Mike has the craziest problem with raccoons in his yard; wait 'til you hear what they've done now." "Didn't you go to France last year? Tell Stacey about that cool place to eat."

When Kids Are Coming

I love kids and I love to have them at parties; they bring an energy and freshness that's always a party pick-me-up. But a party that includes small children is definitely different from an adult party—the food, the pacing, everything changes when parents need to keep an eye on their kids.

Here's a secret: The best way to incorporate little ones into a party is actually to separate them. Let's face it, they think we're boring, and unless a clingy child *wants* to hang on her mother's arm, it's a good idea to provide optional entertainment for the young—a craft table, a movie to watch, some outdoor games to play, a room with some toys in it. They'll feel more comfortable, and you won't worry about whether they're whining in their parents' ears that they want to go home.

Plan food kids like, too. Have a snack table with small sandwiches, carrot sticks, crackers, cookies, etc. Keep some chicken nuggets in the fridge in case they hate everything you're serving for dinner, and you can microwave a customized little meal for them.

When everyone gathers together for the meal itself, don't ignore the children. Ask them about their lives and opinions (which are frequently more fascinating than Margo-from-the-office's latest divorce stories). Go around the table and see how many riddles the grown-ups can remember from their childhoods. Parents will especially appreciate it if you show an interest in their kids.

> ## * Joni's Favorites *
>
> A set of stainless steel bowls is a must-have. Get a set big enough to hold salad for an army. Time and again you will use them for mixing party-sized foods, double batches of dough, and even for holding crushed ice beneath another bowl of shrimp.

Spontaneous Parties

I like these best. There are no expectations, so it doesn't matter if your ice cubes are frozen in a solid chunk, or if you run out of potato chips and somebody has to dash to the store. Everybody knows it's on the fly, and they're relaxed and sympathetic, eager to help you throw things together at the last minute. You can cook like a madwoman and toss things here and there in the kitchen, and it's all in casual good humor. (You would still probably do this for dressy parties, only then it looks hysterical instead of carefree.) Spontaneous parties can often be the most fun of all—everyone's in an adventurous mood and ready to have a good time, rather than squished into dress shoes that pinch or worried about which fork to pick up first.

Tip

Let salsa save you: Add it to cooked rice for a quick Spanish rice dish, add it to mayonnaise for a fast salad dressing, add it to meat loaf to make it moist and tasty, pour it over a brick of cream cheese and serve with crackers for a fast appetizer.

As busy as we all are these days, sometimes it's nearly impossible to coordinate more than two people's schedules, and a spontaneous get-together is often the only way it will work. Just ask everyone if they want to come over and make funnel cakes (recipe on p. 267), or help you make pizza, or watch a new movie together. These impromptu gatherings sometimes end up being some of our fondest memories.

Showers

Bridal and baby showers are always festive celebrations of a happy event, and a great opportunity for women to socialize (we never chat enough, do we?). The easiest way to throw one is to enlist help. One person sends out the invitations and handles the RSVPs, another one brings a veggie platter, another one brings the cake, another one's in charge of games and prizes, another one handles the group gift if there is one, and so on. You clean the house, set up chairs, decorate, and put out a pretty tablecloth and dishes (or if it's a huge gathering, paper plates). You can make it a brunch, a luncheon, or simply a party with cake.

And don't forget something to drink. Here are some yummy punch and slush recipes your guests will love:

TROPICAL SLUSH

    4 bananas, mashed with mixer
    1 (12 oz.) can frozen lemonade concentrate
    1 (12 oz.) can frozen orange juice concentrate
    1 (46 oz.) can pineapple juice
    1¼ cups sugar
    6 cups water
    2 (2 liter) bottles 7-Up

Mix all ingredients except the 7-Up. Pour into 2 nine-by-twelve-inch loaf pans. Freeze. Remove from freezer 1½ hours before needed and place in punch bowl to thaw. At serving time, add 1½ bottles 7-Up and mix all together.

HOT CIDER PUNCH

    1 gallon apple cider
    2 (8 oz.) cans frozen orange juice concentrate
    3 whole cloves
    3 whole cinnamon sticks

Place cider and orange juice in large soup pot over high heat. Tie cloves and cinnamon in a cheesecloth pouch and add to pot. Bring mixture to boiling, then reduce heat and simmer 30 minutes.

REFRESHING PUNCH

2 cups sugar

2 cups water

⅔ cup lemon juice

2 (6 oz.) cans orange juice concentrate

2 quarts water

1 teaspoon vanilla extract

1 teaspoon almond extract

Yellow food coloring, if desired

1 (2 liter) bottle ginger ale

Combine and serve.

ORANGE-PINEAPPLE PUNCH

1 (14 oz.) can sweetened condensed milk

1 (46 oz.) can pineapple juice, chilled

1 (2 liter) bottle orange soda, chilled

½ gallon orange sherbet

Stir first three ingredients in a punch bowl. Float scoops of sherbet in bowl and serve.

LUAU PUNCH

1 (46 oz.) can pineapple juice

1 large can guava nectar

1 large can papaya nectar

1 quart ginger ale

½ gallon lime sherbet

Combine and serve.

FRUITY SLUSH

2 (15 oz.) cans fruit cocktail

2 (15 oz.) cans mandarin oranges

1 (15 oz.) can pineapple chunks

1 (28 oz.) can pears

1 (28 oz.) can peaches

5 bananas

3 cups strawberries

1 cup sugar

2 (2 liter) bottles 7-Up

Drain juice from canned fruits. Pour fruit into large saucepan and add sugar. Boil, then cool. Peel bananas. Slice bananas and strawberries and add to mixture. Freeze. When ready to serve, fill glass half with fruit, then add 7-Up.

JELL-O PUNCH

2 cups heated pineapple juice

1 (3 oz.) package lime gelatin (or any flavor)

2 (2 liter) bottles 7-Up

1 (6 oz.) can frozen limeade concentrate (or whatever flavor that matches gelatin)

Dissolve gelatin in heated pineapple juice. Mix with other ingredients and serve.

Here are four tips to keep in mind when making punch:

1. When combining ice cream and soda, put the ice cream in last to minimize foam.

2. When pouring soda, which tends to glug and splash slowly from the bottle, swirl the bottle around to create an air tunnel down the middle and the soda will pour smoothly and quickly.

3. To make any punch a pretty pastel, drop in scoops of vanilla ice cream.

4. To tint a punch pink, add the juice from a bottle of maraschino cherries.

Easy Menus

Don't forget to plan the appearance, as well as the taste, of the food you serve—include a variety of colors and textures to make meals appealing. Here are several extra-easy menus that you can use for all kinds of gatherings. Each includes no-recipe ideas, such as a chopped fruit salad; another dish that can be made ahead; and simple recipes you can find in the back of the book, which are indicated with an asterisk.

Winter Dinner

* Clam chowder (make the day before, warm up to serve)

Apricot-glazed pork roast (just spread a jar of apricot jam over a pork roast before you cook it)

Buttery brussels sprouts (steam or boil the sprouts, toss with butter and celery seed)

Rice with almonds (pick a yummy packaged rice pilaf, cook it in chicken broth instead of water, and add toasted slivered almonds)

Cinnamon cake (prepare that morning)

After-Sledding Party

Ham 'n' cheese melts (spread garlic mayonnaise or mustard on toasted submarine rolls, top with ham and cheese, broil 'til bubbly)

Cole slaw (make the night before—shred a head of green cabbage, 1 carrot, ¼ head of red cabbage, place in bowl; pour bottled cole slaw dressing over all, cover and chill overnight)

Tip: Look for pre-cut packages of shredded cole slaw mix in the produce aisle.

Heated apple cider

* Corn casserole (make it that morning, warm up later)

Pineapple bar cookies (made ahead, frozen, then thawed)

Valentine's Dinner Party

* Beef Stroganoff

Pasta (look for heart-shaped pasta, boil it, and serve Stroganoff over drained pasta)

Green beans (steam, then toss with butter and thyme)

* Baked stuffed tomato (while it bakes you can pay attention to the Stroganoff)

* Strawberry cake (bake that morning, in heart-shaped pans if you wish)

Purchased chocolate truffles

Listen to Your Mother!

Setting a table should be a creative endeavor, and the final result should please the eye before you ever sit down. Taking care to fold napkins in a festive way—even if you only tie a bow around them—makes the table just that much more welcoming. Use fairly stiff cloth napkins so they will hold their shape, and make sure the napkins are large—sixteen square inches or more. Here are some simple napkin-folding techniques:

Utensil pocket: Fold your napkin in half, then in half again, forming a square. Bring one of the open points down to form a pocket and fold back the sides underneath. Rest the napkin on the table with points up and down, and utensils tucked into pocket.

Scroll: Roll up a stiff napkin from one point to the other, bend in half, and place in goblet. (This is especially effective if you use two napkins in contrasting colors, to form stripes.) Instead of placing it in a goblet, you can tie it around the middle and rest it next to the forks. (A basketful of these, points up, are great for casual get-togethers.)

Fan: Simply fold the napkin back and forth in one-inch pleats, and slip a napkin ring into the center position.

Cone shape: Fold napkin in half, then roll from one end on an angle to form a cone. Turn cone point side up and fold down exterior layer of fabric to keep cone from unrolling. Place on plate or table.

Standard formal: Simply pull the center of the napkin through a ring, then pull the top and bottom parts to make them full and fanned out.

Water lily: Fold each of the four corners in to the middle, forming a diamond. Turn over carefully and fold new corners in to the middle. Turn over again and fold corners in one last time. Pull points of napkin up to keep design in place.

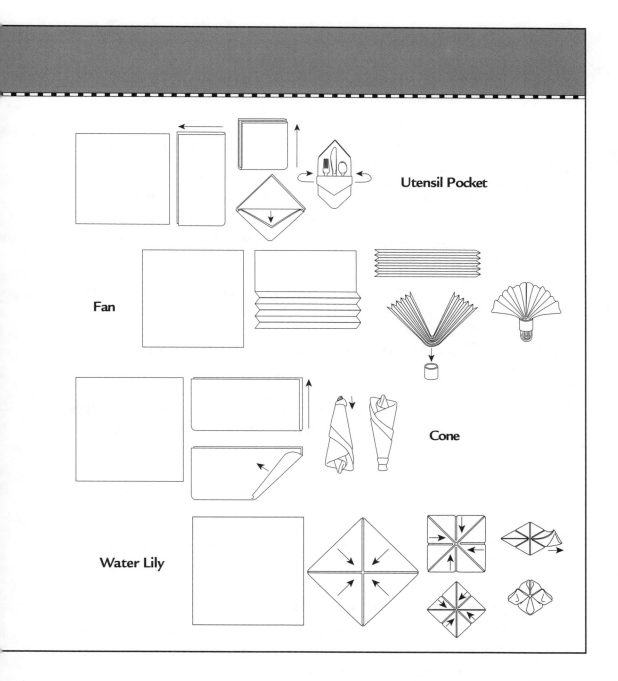

Utensil Pocket

Fan

Cone

Water Lily

Spring Supper

Garden greens with berry dressing (whisk ½ cup seedless raspberry jam with ½ cup poppy-seed dressing)

* Macadamia-crusted salmon

New potatoes (choose tiny ones and boil in skins; toss with butter and garlic)

Asian stir-fried vegetables (cut strips of veggies, including bright strips of red and yellow peppers, maybe some snow peas, and stir-fry in a mixture of oil, soy sauce, and freshly grated ginger)

* Lemon tarts (make crusts and curd the day before; fill as you serve them)

Too Hot to Cook Summer Luncheon Buffet

* Chicken salad (make the day before)

Fruit medley (simply chop up seasonal fruits—melons, grapes, and berries make a nice combination)

* Pesto rice salad (make the day before)

Cold shrimp (place on platter of crushed ice, and serve a tangy shrimp sauce on the side)

* Peach pie with ice cream (make in early morning while it's still cool)

Special Friends Dinner

Pear and bleu cheese salad (mix greens with sliced pear, crumbled bleu cheese, and purchased candied walnuts or pecans; toss with a light vinaigrette dressing)

Tri-tip roast (buy already cooked and packaged; microwave for seven minutes—moist, delicious, perfectly seasoned)

Glazed carrots (cook whole baby carrots in an inch of water or apple juice, plus a stick of butter and a cup of brown sugar, until fork-tender)

* Creamy polenta

* Flourless chocolate cake and raspberries

Fourth of July Buffet

Red, white & blue salad (toss blueberries, strawberries, and slices of banana—keep banana white with a sprinkling of Fruit Fresh; serve alone, or over greens)

Watermelon wedges

* Potato salad

Grilled chicken or burgers

* Lunchmeat roll-ups

Flag stripes torte (layer horizontal slices of pound cake and strawberry ice cream in a loaf pan the day before; freeze—slice vertically to serve, and top with whipped cream and blueberries to make the flag's stars)

Fiesta Brunch

* Quiche with avocado/tomato salsa

* Fajita salad

* Chili rice

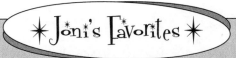

✳ Joni's Favorites ✳

A tortilla warmer is not only for those who eat a lot of Mexican food, but is great for heating any food (muffins!) you want to keep warm, yet don't want to dry out. You'll think of dozens of uses!

Tortilla chips and salsa for dipping

* Cinnamon crème brûlées

After/During the Big Game

* Hot artichoke dip (serve with crackers)

Crunchy vegetable platter (carrot sticks, celery sticks, jicama, cherry tomatoes, broccoli florets)

Pizza dogs (roll franks in pizza sauce, then grated mozzarella cheese; encase in strips of purchased pizza dough and bake until golden)

* Cowboy beans 'n' bacon (make earlier and chill, then warm in oven)

* Orange rolls

* Pecan squares (make the day before)

Autumn Brunch

* Apple-topped oven pancakes

* Harvest frittata

Maple bacon strips (drizzle bacon with maple syrup and a twist of fresh ground pepper while cooking)

Pear & yam bake

* Pumpkin bread (serve with soft cream cheese)

Harvest Dinner Party

* Pumpkin soup

* Lamb shanks

Mashed potatoes

* Portobello mushrooms stuffed with spinach

Green peas and pearl onions, steamed and tossed with toasted pecans

* Apple pie

How to Impress Your Parents

When Mom and Dad are coming for dinner, you want to surprise them with something showy, or at least something so delicious they'll want the recipe! But don't agonize over this dinner; your parents will still love you even if nothing turns out right and you have to hop in the car for takeout.

You'll also want to avoid getting so gourmet and so exotic that your parents won't like the food; many parents aren't ready for squid, and you know your own parents—would they be just as happy with a good meat loaf? A simple, hearty dinner is often the way to go, then you can wow them with dessert.

Perhaps your mom would appreciate it if you tried to make some of the favorites she cooked as you were growing up—use some of her old recipes and let her know how much you appreciate them.

Here are some dishes that are easy to prepare, but just special enough to impress your folks with your cooking skills (recipes are in the back of this book):

Homemade granola (if they're staying over)

Easy sticky ring (also great for breakfast)

Breakfast casserole (made the night before)

Cheddar & herb biscuits

Roast lamb

"Barbecued" chicken (baked in the oven)

Pasta with tomato-basil sauce

Shrimp on rosemary skewers

Steak (insert your name here)

Chicken pizza roulade

Crab bisque

Roast chicken

Spicy steak

Killer cheesecake

English fish 'n' chips

Key lime pie

Cheeseburger soup

Sweet & spicy scallops

Check the recipes in the back of the book; you'll find some great basics that will make you a confident cook, and some easy show stoppers that will definitely wow your parents.

Chapter Fourteen

Breakfasts in a Hurry

We've all heard the following, right? "A balanced breakfast." "Part of this nutritious breakfast." "Fuel for the day." "Brain food." From all sides, we're getting advice to start the day right and eat something besides empty calories, something that will help us sustain top performance.

Well, we know it's not a donut. We can convince ourselves that it's apple pie (after all, apples are fruit, the crust is made from grain, and whipped cream is a dairy product containing protein), but we know we deserve better.

It's just that preparing a well-balanced breakfast seems too time-consuming. We're not in the mood for warmed-up leftovers from last night, even if they do contain vegetables, meat, and lots of minerals. It's just not breakfasty. So how can we eat right when we're in a hurry?

First of all, slow down. If you find you're dashing out of the house before you can pump some energy into your body, maybe you're sleeping in too late. Sacrifice ten or fifteen minutes of sleep for a moment of healthy eating in the morning. Don't live from one cup of coffee to the next, just trying to stay awake. Eat foods that perk you up and get you started without caffeine.

Instead of letting your appetite rule you, let you rule your appetite. You really can train your body to hunger for the right things in the morning. If you've gotten into the sugar-and-carbohydrate habit, gradually ease off until you can eat a scoop of egg-and-tuna salad or a slice of meat instead of a bowl of sugar-coated Snapperoos. Enjoy a piece of cheese and some fruit, and munch on pretzels for carbohydrates.

> ✳ **Joni's Favorites** ✳
>
> **The creamiest oatmeal is Mc-Cann's Irish oatmeal. Get the one in the box, not the can. It's rough-cut oatmeal, but mixes up beautifully.**

Car Munchies

If you find yourself grabbing a Pop-Tart as you jump into the car, reach instead for a piece of fruit. Keep napkins or paper towels in the car, and throw a towel over your lap to protect your clothes (who will know?).

Or keep munchies right in the car. Why not? As long as they're not perishable, all kinds of snacks can be stored in a small container beside the driver's seat. Think of the things campers nosh on: beef sticks, crackers, granola bars, dried fruit. Any of these are better for you than the high-fat, high-sugar breakfasts advertised during Saturday morning cartoons.

Packing a Week Ahead

We pack lunches to make it easier on ourselves, right? It's virtually impossible to prepare a lunch in most workplaces or schools, so we tote one along. Why can't we put as much forethought into breakfast? I'm not saying you have to carry it with you, but if you make up five breakfasts on the weekend, your weekday mornings will be a breeze—you'll save time thinking about what to have and assembling it, and you'll eat more nutritiously. You'll get out of the boring rut of eating the exact same thing each morning, too.

All you need are five Tupperware containers. Start by making a list of every good breakfast food you enjoy. If you like pizza for breakfast—or whatever else—put that on the list too. Now choose two or three items that represent a balance of grains, proteins, and fruits, and assign each one to a day. Here's an example:

Monday: Yogurt mixed with granola and fruit

Tuesday: Scrambled eggs, a bagel and fruit-flavored cream cheese, such as peach, strawberry, or pineapple.

Wednesday: Ham and cheese on toast, orange sections

Thursday: Vegetarian quiche, melon chunks

Friday: Blueberry waffles, sausage

On a weekend morning or afternoon, prepare and pack each breakfast separately, then store in the freezer or the fridge for the week ahead.

Monday's yogurt is already in its own container. Pour ½ cup granola into a resealable sandwich bag and attach it to the yogurt carton with a rubber band. Place chopped fruit in a plastic container, then store all three together in the fridge.

On Monday morning, stir everything into the plastic container, which will serve as your bowl. (This concoction is a Swiss favorite called *Birchermuesli,* by the way.)

To prepare for Tuesday, scramble some eggs and put them in a plastic container with a cream-cheese-covered bagel. This will store nicely in the fridge. Then, Tuesday morning, heat the whole thing up in the microwave until the eggs are steaming hot again.

Tip

Make omelettes and scrambled eggs healthier by using more whites and fewer yolks.

On Wednesday, you're having ham and cheese on toast with orange sections. On your preparation day, toast your bread slices and place a slice of ham and a slice of cheese between them. Put in plastic container. Peel an orange and add the orange sections to your container. Chill. On Wednesday morning, take out the sandwich and broil it until the cheese is bubbly and the toast is crispy again. The orange sections are all set to eat.

For Thursday's breakfast, chop up some melon chunks and save them in a plastic container. Then, Thursday morning, simply microwave a slice of already-made quiche (purchased or homemade), and you're set.

Make a batch of blueberry waffles (or pancakes) ahead of time for Friday (and for future days). Freeze them in resealable bags holding two each. Put one package in a plastic container with cooked sausage. On the day you want this breakfast, just pop the waffles in the toaster until they're hot, and heat the sausage in the microwave.

You'll come up with dozens of other possibilities, including the leftover shrimp linguini you brought home in a restaurant doggie bag. You might even have such wonderful breakfasts that you can cut down at lunchtime and knock off a few pounds before that trip to the beach!

Grab 'n' Go Strategies

No matter how organized you are, some mornings get crazy—the power goes out, the kids' shoes are missing, and you find yourself running at top speed. Sometimes you'll need to grab an emergency packet and go. These are easy to make ahead of time and freeze, for those hectic mornings when there really isn't time to slow down. Usually, by the time you arrive at your destination, the items have thawed and you can gulp down, at least, a little nutrition.

Fruit pops—Use high-quality fruit juice (or pureed fruit) and freeze it in popsicle forms or plastic cups with a plastic spoon for the handle. Slide the handle through the center of a paper towel to catch drips, and it's just like eating a fresh piece of fruit.

Tortilla wraps—Spread a flavored cream cheese over a tortilla, then slices of cheese and lunch meat. Roll up tightly, and chill in plastic wrap. Slice into one-inch pinwheel segments, then freeze each separately for grabbing on the run.

Trail mix—This freezes wonderfully; simply pour a cupful into a resealable plastic bag, and pop it in the freezer.

Cheese and fruit—Freeze cubes of cheese along with fresh grapes in a resealable sandwich bag. Because these are small items, they'll thaw quickly when you grab a bag and go.

Pizza muffins—Make a whole batch and freeze them individually. Spread pizza sauce onto English muffin halves, then sprinkle with grated mozzarella. Bake until bubbly, then freeze, tightly wrapped.

Mini-sandwiches—Spread a bagel or two slices of bread with one of these easy spreads, then wrap in plastic and freeze (these are also good if you're heading off to the soccer game and there isn't time to stop for dinner):

> cream cheese and chopped olives
> peanut butter and jam
> cream cheese, basil, and chopped roasted red peppers
> ricotta cheese mixed with tuna
> butter mixed with herbs and chopped meat
> cream cheese and minced dried fruit

Cracker creations—Package several cheese and cracker "sandwiches," and freeze three or four in one bag. Add lunchmeat if you like.

Frozen patties—A cold hamburger patty is not the worst thing in the world, especially if you're hungry. And it thaws fairly quickly. But also consider salmon patties, crab and tuna patties, ham patties, and potato-cheese patties.

Cold pizza—Freeze individual slices (and then, if you do have a minute to spare, you can zap in the microwave).

Slices of quick bread—Freeze moist slices of pumpkin bread, banana bread, even pound cake, for grabbing on the run.

Easy-Fix Breakfasts

Even if all you have is a few minutes, that's enough time to prepare a delicious breakfast for your family. Here are some easy recipes to make that first meal of the day a real treat:

BREAKFAST BURRITOS

   3 tablespoons butter

   2 cups cooked potatoes, chopped (or use frozen hash browns)

   ½ cup chopped onion

   5 eggs, beaten

   1 (4.5 oz.) can chopped mild green chilies

   1 cup shredded cheddar cheese

   6 flour tortillas

In a large skillet, melt butter and sauté potatoes and onion until tender. Add eggs, chilies, and cheddar cheese, stirring until eggs are cooked.

   Wrap tortillas in paper towels and microwave for 1 minute, or until softened and warm. Fill with egg mixture, folding tortilla to encase filling.

   Makes 6.

WHEAT BERRIES

You'll need to start this the night before, but once you get hooked, you'll want this every morning (and it's so filling that you won't get the mid-morning munchies, either).

   ⅔ cup winter wheat (whole grains)

   2 cups water

   Brown sugar

   Milk or cream

Place wheat and water in a Crock-Pot or slow cooker on the lowest setting and let cook overnight. The next day, remove the softened grains with a slotted spoon, and serve in cereal bowls. Top with brown sugar and milk. (Chilled wheat berries are also a great salad ingredient!)

   Makes 3 to 4 servings.

POTATO-CRUST QUICHE

This is good when you have at least an hour.

16 oz. frozen hash brown potatoes, thawed
½ cup butter, melted
2 cups shredded cheddar-jack cheese
1 cup diced cooked ham
½ cup evaporated milk
3 eggs
½ teaspoon black pepper
Dash of salt

Preheat oven to 425 degrees. Press potatoes into a greased pie plate to form a crust. Drizzle with melted butter. Bake for 25 minutes.

Sprinkle crust with half the cheese, half the ham, then the remaining cheese and the remaining ham.

In a small bowl, whisk milk, eggs, pepper, and salt. Pour over ham and cheese. Reduce oven temperature to 350 degrees and bake quiche for another 30 minutes.

Makes 4 to 6 servings.

BREAKFAST PIZZA

½ lb. sausage
½ cup chopped onion
4 eggs
1 prepared pizza crust, such as Boboli*
2 tomatoes, chopped
2 cups shredded mozarella cheese

In a large skillet, brown sausage with onions until sausage is crumbly. Pour off drippings and spoon sausage mixture onto pizza crust.

In same pan, scramble eggs and cook until set. Spoon onto pizza. Sprinkle with chopped tomatoes and cheese. Place under broiler for 2 minutes or until cheese is bubbly. Slice into wedges and serve.

You can also use the quick-pizza-crust mixes available at the super-market, or make your own pizza crust from scratch.

Makes 6 to 8 servings.

Tip: Keep pizza crust crispy by putting the cheese on first, instead of last.

BREAKFAST TRIFLE

    1 angel food cake, torn into bite-sized pieces
    2 cups lemon yogurt
    1 cup granola
    2 cups fresh fruit, sliced
    2 cups fat-free whipped topping

Layer ⅓ of each ingredient in a clear trifle bowl, in order shown. Repeat two more times. Chill.

Makes 6 to 8 servings.

OMELETTES

This is one of the fastest, heartiest breakfasts you can make—two minutes, and you're done. For lower-cholesterol omelettes, use three egg whites, omitting yolks.

    2 teaspoons butter
    2 eggs
    1 teaspoon water
    Salt and pepper to taste

Heat butter in skillet or omelette pan over high heat. Whisk eggs with water and pour into skillet, swirling quickly (the trick to making good omelettes is to cook them fast over high heat). Lift sections of the omelette with a spatula to allow uncooked portions to flow beneath. Add salt and pepper. Add fillings as desired. Fold over and slide onto serving plate. Repeat to make additional omelettes.

Terrific omelette fillings:

Grated cheese, any kind

Cooked, crumbled bacon and sour cream

Chopped spinach and sautéed onion

Crab and roasted red peppers

Chopped artichoke hearts and jack cheese

Shrimp and asparagus

Tomato salsa, chilies, and cheddar cheese

Diced ham and shredded Swiss cheese

Onions, peppers, and sausage

Minced herbs

Flakes of salmon and fresh dill

Olives, tomatoes, and Parmesan cheese

Dash of pizza sauce and mozzarella cheese

Seafood and diced avocado

Mushrooms and minced shallots

Pine nuts, pesto sauce, and Romano cheese

CRAB-MELT MUFFINS

6 English muffins, split
1 (6 oz.) can white crab meat
2 cups shredded Colby-jack cheese
2 green onions, finely chopped
Mayonnaise to moisten

Heat broiler. Place English muffins cut side up on a baking sheet. In a medium bowl, stir crab meat, cheese, and green onions with enough mayonnaise to moisten. Spread mixture on muffins and broil until bubbly, about 2 minutes. (These may also be baked at 350 degrees for a softer version, just until cheese melts, about 10 minutes.)

Makes 6 servings (two muffins per serving).

"BANANAS FOSTER" PANCAKES

Keep in mind that you can substitute pineapple, blueberries, strawberries, applesauce, or a zillion other fruits for the bananas in the topping.

Pancakes:
Nonstick cooking spray
1 cup buttermilk
1 mashed ripe banana
2 tablespoons cooking oil
1 egg, beaten
1 teaspoon vanilla (or try rum flavoring)
1 cup flour
1 tablespoon sugar
1 teaspoon baking powder
½ teaspoon baking soda
½ teaspoon salt

Preheat an oil-sprayed skillet or griddle over medium heat. In a large bowl, mix wet ingredients, then add dry ones. Pour 3- to 4-inch circles onto skillet and turn when edges appear dry.

Topping:
3 bananas, peeled and sliced
½ cup butter
½ cup brown sugar
½ cup pecans
Whipped cream (optional)

Stir all ingredients in a saucepan over medium heat until sugar dissolves and bananas soften slightly. Pour over pancakes. Top with whipped cream, if desired.

Makes 4 servings.

BACON 'N' EGG SQUARES

6 eggs
¾ cup sour cream
1 cup cooked, crumbled bacon
1 green onion, chopped
1 teaspoon tarragon
½ cup shredded Swiss cheese
2 tablespoons butter, melted

Preheat oven to 350 degrees. Butter a 9-inch square baking dish. In a large bowl, beat eggs until fluffy. Add sour cream, bacon, onion, tarragon, cheese, and butter. Pour into pan. Bake 20 to 25 minutes, then cut into squares.

Makes 6 to 8 servings.

Chapter Fifteen

Gifts from
the Kitchen

treats from the kitchen make ideal gifts, even for folks who are "hard to buy for," because we all need to eat! You don't need to know someone's taste in music or decorating, or what size they are—a loaf of bread or a jar of jam is always a perfect fit. Like money, it's something everyone can use. But, unlike money, it's more personal: It shows you cared and invested a bit of yourself in the present. Homemade goodies are also impossible to buy, so take pride in presenting your one-of-a-kind memento, whether it's a holiday remembrance, a birthday surprise, or a hostess gift. (And be sure to check the back of this book for additional recipes that would make delicious presents!)

Edible Goodies

Here are some great ideas for delicious gifts. Give one of these to a special person or family; or adapt to suit a friend's specific tastes. Either way, you are giving a wonderful, personalized gift!

Honey

A jar of honey is a great gift to keep on hand since it doesn't spoil. Specialty honeys such as French lavender honey or orange blossom honey are always appreciated. Tie on a wooden honey dipper or a little teddy bear to make it more of a gift than a grocery item. (Honey with homemade bread would be to die for!)

Pasta Basket

Line a pasta bowl or basket with a red gingham cloth, then fill it with the ingredients for a spaghetti dinner—a bag of pasta, a jar of homemade or purchased sauce, a pasta fork, pesto sauce, pine nuts, freshly grated Parmesan cheese, a meatballer (yes, there are scoops for making meatballs), a cruet of Italian dressing, focaccia bread—whatever fits in your container.

PESTO SAUCE

2 cups packed fresh basil
1 cup olive oil
½ cup pine nuts
⅓ cup freshly grated Parmesan cheese
3 cloves crushed garlic
1 teaspoon salt

(recipe continues)

Blend all ingredients in a food processor or blender. Store in a covered container in refrigerator.

Makes 2 cups.

Farm-Fresh Basket

There's something beautiful about eggs: Picture a bounteous basket of pure white eggs (or mix in some brown ones) nestled in a linen tea towel with a jar of marmalade, some fresh muffins, and a crock of creamy butter. Other goodies to tuck in for a great breakfast include bacon or sausage, cheeses, herbal teas. This is also a great collection to present in an omelette pan.

Cozy Cocoa Collection

How about two mugs, two packets of instant cocoa mix, and a big bag of marshmallows all tied up with ribbon? What a great winter warm-up. If a couple is hosting you for several days, add

a snuggly blanket or some firewood. (To make your own cocoa mix, see the following recipe.)

INSTANT COCOA MIX

> 1 (8 quarts) package nonfat dry-milk powder
> 1 (16 oz.) can cocoa
> 1 lb. sifted powdered sugar
> 1 (6 oz.) jar powdered non-dairy creamer

Thoroughly mix all ingredients and store in an airtight container that will hold 15 cups. For gifts, package individual servings in cellophane bags with instructions, e.g., ¼ cup of the mix is one serving when mixed with ¾ cup boiling water.

Ice Cream Rescue Kit

You'll need to buy part of this (the ice cream) on the way to your friend's house, but how about a basket containing an ice-cream scoop, glass parfait dishes or malt glasses, and an assortment of ice-cream toppings? Don't forget the sprinkles!

Remember the Kids

Sometimes the most appreciated gesture is to remember your host's children. Put together a gift bag of cookies, M&M's, puzzles, bubbles, toys, and books, and watch their eyes light up.

Cookie-of-the-Month

A promise to deliver fresh, chewy cookies every month for the next year makes a wonderful gift. Vary the kinds and pack them up in cute tins.

Home-Grown Herbs

These make a particularly touching gift, as you grew the herbs yourself. All you need is a sunny windowsill and a few small pots of herbs. Snip some fresh ones, tie with a thin ribbon, and your friend has a fragrant garni bundle (a packet of herbs to simmer) to flavor everything from soups to roasts. Or, give an entire plant with a bow tied around the container.

✳ Joni's Favorites ✳

Herbs de Provence is a great blend of delicious flavors that work on everything from meats to bread dough.

Flavored Butters

These are so easy to make, yet so appreciated. Simply soften a cup of butter, mash with 1–2 tablespoons fresh minced herbs, then pack in a crock and chill. If you have some pretty butter molds, press the butter into those, then pop it out once it's chilled. Remember to present your butter in an attractive container. The following are both sweet and savory additions for making flavored butters:

Tarragon	Minced carrot
Fennel	Minced onion
Basil	Minced bell pepper
Oregano	Minced chilies
Thyme	Lemon pepper
Chopped cilantro	Worcestershire sauce
Pickle relish	Minced dried fruit
Chopped olives	Minced apple

Crushed garlic

Minced celery

Chopped pimiento

Crushed capers

Ethnic spice blends

Cinnamon

Honey

Toasted ground nuts

Pesto sauce

Crushed pineapple

Coconut

Coarse ground pepper

Celery seed

Bacon bits

Sesame seeds

Shelled sunflower seeds

Citrus zest

Parsely, snipped

Salsa & Chips

Tuck a jar of homemade salsa into a basket, then some packages of gourmet corn chips—easy, festive, fun.

- -

HOMEMADE SALSA

Be sure to keep this refrigerated, and use it within a day or two.

2 tomatoes, peeled and diced (blanch tomatoes and the
   peel will slip right off)

¼ red onion, chopped

1 jalapeño or Anaheim chili, seeded and chopped (omit for
   a milder version)

1 green onion, chopped

2 tablespoons chopped cilantro

1 teaspoon crushed garlic

Juice of 1 lime

Salt and pepper to taste

Mix all ingredients and store in refrigerator in lidded container. (Be adventurous—experiment with mango, pineapple, kiwi, or papaya in place of one tomato.)

Makes 1½ cups.

Dried Fruit

This is easy to keep on hand; when you need a present, just fill a glass jar with bright strips of delicious fruit (especially welcome in winter, when fruits are out of season). They're also great combined with nuts and pretzels to make a trail mix.

To dry fruit, slice it thinly and arrange on a baking sheet. Bake in a low oven (200 degrees) for several hours or until fruit is dry. The following are good fruits to slice and dry:

Apples

Bananas

Oranges (great for simmering in apple cider with some cinnamon sticks)

Pineapple

Apricots

Cherries

Cranberries

Dates

Figs

Mango

Papaya

Candy

CHOCOLATE BARK

Nothing could be easier, yet this candy is always a huge hit. Simply melt a package of white-, milk-, or dark-chocolate chips in the top of a double boiler over simmering water, then stir in a cupful of the following:

Crisped rice cereal

Coconut

Raisins

Marshmallows

Nuts

Crushed peppermint candies

Crushed pretzels

Peanut-butter chips

Smooth mixture onto waxed paper and let harden. Break into pieces. Candy bark is especially pretty if you swirl together two colors of chocolate when pouring it onto the waxed paper.

Makes 3 cups of candy.

- -

PRALINES

My Louisiana-born husband would want me to tell you how to pronounce this the proper way: It isn't pray-leens; it's prah-leens, honey.

2 cups butter

2 cups sugar

2 cups dark brown sugar

3 tablespoons water

5 cups whipping cream

3 tablespoons vanilla

2 cups shelled whole pecans

1 cup crushed pecans

In a large skillet over medium-high heat, stir butter, sugars, and water for 3 minutes. Add cream and ground pecans and bring to a boil. Stir about 15 minutes until candy thermometer reads 234 degrees (soft ball stage). Add vanilla and whole pecans, continuing to stir until temperature reaches 260 degrees (hard ball stage). Now spoon small amounts onto waxed paper and let harden in 3-inch round puddles.

These would make a fun addition to a Mardi Gras gift basket, with Cajun seasonings tucked in as well.

Makes 2 dozen "prah-leens."

PUMPKIN FUDGE

Top each cut square with a small candy pumpkin or a candy corn to make this a Halloween goodie.

> 1 cup milk
> 3 cups sugar
> ½ cup canned solid pumpkin
> 3 tablespoons corn syrup
> Dash of salt
> 1 teaspoon pumpkin pie spice
> 1½ teaspoons vanilla
> 4 ounces (½ stick) butter
> ½ cup chopped nuts

In a medium saucepan, bring first four ingredients to a boil. Reduce heat to medium and continue to boil until mixture reaches 230 degrees on candy thermometer (almost soft ball stage). Remove from heat and stir in remaining ingredients. Let cool to 100 degrees. Beat until thickened, then pour into buttered 8-inch square pan. Chill, then cut into squares.

Makes approximately 3 dozen.

HOMEMADE TAFFY

This is a wonderful, old-fashioned treat—why not be known for this in the neighborhood? It's also fun for party guests to participate in a taffy pull.

1 cup sugar

¾ cup corn syrup

⅔ cup water

2 tablespoons butter

1 tablespoon cornstarch

1 teaspoon salt

1 teaspoon vanilla

2 teaspoons another extract (choose whatever flavor you wish—strawberry, orange, peppermint, almond, etc.)

10 drops food coloring (match the flavor you've chosen)

In a large saucepan, stir sugar, corn syrup, water, butter, cornstarch, and salt until boiling. Continue to stir until candy thermometer reads 256 degrees (hard ball stage). This should take about 20 minutes.

Remove from heat; stir in vanilla, flavoring, and coloring. Pour into a buttered 8-inch square baking dish. Let cool until just warm enough to handle. Butter hands and work taffy until light in color and stiff (fold, stretch, and pull). Form into ropes, then cut with buttered scissors and wrap in small squares of waxed paper, twisting ends.

Makes 3 to 4 dozen pieces of candy.

Nuts and Crunchy Snack Mixes

RAISIN-CRAN CRUNCH

3 cups Chex cereal

1½ cups oatmeal

1 cup chopped nuts

½ cup butter

⅔ cup honey

¼ cup brown sugar

1 teaspoon cinnamon

Dash of salt

½ cup chocolate raisins

½ cup dried cranberries (or chopped dried apricots)

In a large bowl, combine cereal, oatmeal, and nuts. In a small saucepan, heat butter, honey, sugar, cinnamon, and salt until sugar dissolves. Pour over dry mixture and stir until thoroughly mixed. Bake on greased baking sheet at 275 degrees for 45 minutes, stirring every 15 minutes. When done, stir in raisins and cranberries.

Makes 6 cups.

SWEET 'N' SPICY NUTS

You can make delicious candied nuts with this same recipe; just omit the pepper.

1 cup sugar

⅓ cup evaporated milk

1 teaspoon cinnamon

½ teaspoon cayenne pepper

1 teaspoon vanilla

2 cups nuts

In a medium saucepan, bring sugar, milk, cinnamon, and pepper to a full boil and stir for 2 minutes. The mixture will be at a very soft ball stage. Remove from heat. Stir in vanilla and nuts until nuts are well coated. Pour onto waxed paper and let cool. Break into small pieces.

Makes 2 to 3 cups.

WHITE-CHOCOLATE POPCORN

15 cups popped popcorn

2 cups almonds

1 pound white-chocolate chips (or white candy coating for melting)

3 tablespoons cooking oil

Place popcorn and nuts in a large bowl. In top of a double boiler, melt chips with oil; mix with popcorn and nuts. Spread on waxed paper and let set for 2 hours. Break into small pieces and store tightly covered.

Makes 15 cups.

Pastries

Sometimes a plate of cookies or a pie is exactly the gift to take to new neighbors. Be sure to see chapter eighteen for more ideas.

MINT BROWNIES

These are pretty at Christmas or on St. Patrick's Day, as they have a pale green frosting layer under a shiny chocolate coating, or, use raspberry or straw-berry extract instead of mint and tint the layer pink for other times of year!

1 cup butter

3 (1 oz.) squares unsweetened baking chocolate

1½ cups sugar

3 eggs

¾ cup flour

Pinch of salt

2¼ cups powdered sugar

3 tablespoons milk

¼ teaspoon peppermint extract (or another flavor)

5 drops green food coloring

Glaze

⅔ cup semisweet chocolate chips

3 tablespoons butter

Preheat oven to 350 degrees. In the top of a double boiler, place ¾ cup of the butter, setting aside the other ¼ cup. Add chocolate to double boiler, melting with butter. In a separate bowl, beat eggs and sugar until fluffy. Stir in flour and salt. Add chocolate mixture and pour into a greased nine-by-thirteen-inch baking dish. Bake for 20 minutes. Cool.

In a smaller bowl, beat remaining ¼ cup butter until fluffy. Add powdered sugar, milk, extract, and food coloring. Spread over cooled brownies. Chill 1 hour. Melt chocolate and butter to form glaze; spread over brownies. Cool until set.

Makes 20–24 brownies.

MACADAMIA SANDIES

1 cup butter, at room temperature

⅓ cup sugar

2 teaspoons vanilla

2 teaspoons water

2 cups flour

1 cup crushed macadamia nuts

¼ cup powdered sugar

✳ **Joni's Favorites** ✳

If you bake, you'll notice a marked difference between the waxy, less expensive chocolate, and fine European chocolate, such as Callebaut, a Belgian brand. The difference lies not only in the taste, but in the workability.

(recipe continues)

Preheat oven to 325 degrees. In a large mixing bowl, beat butter until fluffy. Add sugar and beat thoroughly. Beat in vanilla and water. Stir in flour and nuts. Shape into 1-inch balls and bake on ungreased baking sheet for 20 minutes. Cool. Roll in powdered sugar (or shake in bag of powdered sugar).

Makes 3 dozen.

OATMEAL-DATE MUFFINS

2 cups oatmeal
2 cups buttermilk
2 eggs
1 cup cooking oil
1 cup brown sugar
1½ cups pitted, chopped dates
2 cups flour
2 teaspoons baking soda
1 teaspoon baking powder
1 teaspoon salt

Muffins will come out better if you don't overbeat; let the dough be fairly lumpy. If your batter doesn't fill all the muffin holes in your tin, fill the empty ones with water to ensure even baking. And, muffins will form round tops if you grease only halfway up the muffin cup.

Tip

In a large mixing bowl, soak oats in buttermilk for 1 hour. Preheat oven to 350 degrees. In a separate bowl, beat eggs, oil, sugar, and dates. Stir into oatmeal mixture. Sift flour, soda, baking powder, and salt into this same mixture. Stir just until moistened. Spoon into 24 greased muffin cups. Bake 20–25 minutes.

Makes 2 dozen.

ROSE CAKE

2⅛ cups sifted flour

3 teaspoons baking powder

1 teaspoon salt

1½ cups sugar

½ cup shortening

1 cup milk

2 medium eggs

1 teaspoon rose-flavored extract

7 drops red food coloring

In a large bowl, combine dry ingredients. Beat in wet ingredients. Pour into 2 round greased and floured cake pans. Bake 30 minutes at 350 degrees. Cool completely, then frost with white or cream-cheese icing. Garnish with real roses or candied rose petals, if desired.

Soup Mixes

Combine the pasta, beans, and dry seasonings of your favorite soup along with instructions for how much broth or liquid to add and how to cook it all into soup. This makes an especially pretty gift if the ingredients are layered in colorful stripes in a clear jar.

Preserves and Sauces

EASY JALAPEÑO JELLY

This will keep in the fridge for three months—try it on crackers with cream cheese. (And be sure not to touch your eyes when handling hot peppers. I recommend using plastic gloves so you won't be as likely to touch your eyes and get pepper juice in them. Then discard the gloves for easy cleanup.)

> 2 (12 oz.) jars apple jelly
> 1 red jalapeño pepper
> 1 green jalapeño pepper
> 2 tablespoons cider vinegar

In a small saucepan, melt jelly over low heat. Cut peppers in half, remove seeds, and mince. Stir into jelly. Add vinegar and simmer 5 minutes. Pour into hot, clean jelly jars and chill 1 hour. Stir to evenly distribute minced peppers. Chill completely.

Makes two 12-oz. jars.

FREEZER JAM

This easy recipe calls for strawberries, but you can substitute other berries and fruits. Keep it in the freezer, or in the fridge for two to three weeks.

> 2 quarts strawberries
> ¼ cup lemon juice
> 1 package pectin
> 1 cup corn syrup
> 4½ cups sugar

Mash fruit to yeild 3¼ cups. In a large cooking pot, stir fruit with lemon juice and pectin until well mixed. Let rest 30 minutes. Stir in corn syrup, then sugar. Heat mixture just until sugar dissolves. Pour into clean jars and affix lids. Freeze until ready to use.

Makes 8 cups or 4 pints.

QUICK PICKLES

> 2 lbs. cucumbers, sliced (or the equivalent in baby carrots, blanched)

1 clove garlic

1 tablespoon dill weed

1 pint white vinegar

2 cups sugar

¼ cup pickling salt

Mix all ingredients, cover, and chill for 24 hours.

Makes 6 cups.

TAPENADE

In France and Italy (where it's called olivada), *olives are whipped into a wonderful relish that goes great with pasta, sandwiches, soups—you name it. Here's an easy version:*

1 cup pitted black olives

¾ cup green olives

1 tablespoon olive oil

1 tablespoon lemon juice

1 teaspoon fresh rosemary (or ½ teaspoon dried)

½ teaspoon fennel seeds

Blend all ingredients in food processor or blender until a coarse paste forms. Store in covered container in refrigerator.

Makes 1½ cups.

MUSTARD

If you've never made your own mustard, you're in for a treat—and so are those who receive a jar of your own special blend!

Check specialty markets for various colors of mustard seeds.

1 cup yellow mustard seeds

1 cup dark or black mustard seeds

Water to moisten

2 tablespoons balsamic vinegar   *(recipe continues)*

Salt to taste

¼ cup honey (optional)

2 teaspoons olive oil

½ teaspoon pepper or crushed herbs

Grind mustard seeds with a mortar or with a spice or coffee grinder. Whisk in remaining ingredients (experiment with various herbs and peppers), then store in refrigerator in lidded jar.

Makes 1 cup.

FLAVORED VINEGARS

These are so pretty in a tall, slim bottle—and they're wonderful for tossing with oil to make a delicious salad. Start with a wine vinegar, or one of the following:

White vinegar

Balsamic vinegar

Rice vinegar

Malt vinegar

Raspberry vinegar

Cider vinegar

To one quart of your chosen vinegar, add small amounts, or a couple of sprigs, of the following washed herbs: tarragon, rosemary, dried chiles, citrus slices, berries, basil, garlic, bay leaves, thyme, or mint. Seal the bottle and let the vinegar absorb the herb's flavors for one week.

FLAVORED OILS

Again, as with the vinegars, you can make a beautiful gift by filling a pretty bottle with a good virgin olive oil and some herbs or seasonings— chiles, sun-dried tomatoes, and garlic are all good choices. Also try citrus skins, peppercorns, and fragrant herbs such as rosemary.

Spice Blends

These are always good to use as rubs on meat or to flavor soups and stews. Small jars, fabric pouches, cute envelopes, or even a plastic bag tied with a ribbon make great containers.

TANDOORI

Mix 1½ teaspoons of the following spices:

> ginger
> cumin
> paprika
> garlic powder

with ¾ teaspoon each of these spices:

> cayenne pepper
> coriander
> salt
> tumeric
> cinnamon

Combine all together and store tightly wrapped or in lidded container.

Makes about 3 tablespoons.

TEX-MEX

> 4 tablespoons chili powder
> 2 teaspoons cumin
> 2 teaspoons garlic powder
> 2 teaspoons salt
> 2 teaspoons oregano

Combine all spices and store tightly wrapped or in lidded container.

Makes almost 7 tablespoons or a little more than ⅓ cup.

It's a Wrap

The presentation of your gift is almost as important as the food itself—who wouldn't welcome a pretty basket tied up with cellophane and curls of ribbon? Take a minute to think how you'd like to dress up your present. A brown paper bag can even become a festive wrap if you punch holes near the top and thread them with twine. Stickers or ink-stamped designs also turn a plain bag into a gift wrap.

Scout out fun dishes and bowls at tag sales and thrift shops. For just pennies, you can give your friend a pretty saucer for the butter to go with your muffins. Or a silver butter knife engraved with her initial. How about a glazed crock to hold an herbed butter, or an old-fashioned jar to hold some chili sauce?

Cloth bags are wonderful (and reusable), and are simple to make if you sew. A drawstring tie makes for easy opening and closing. Watch for holiday or seasonal fabric remnants to go on sale, or look for oversized cloth napkins. Even easier: Cut a square of fabric (or a scarf) with pinking shears, then tie up into a loose knot or tie with raffia. A pretty dish towel is also a reusable wrapping.

Get creative with containers. Use flowerpots, mugs, straw hats, Christmas stockings, and china teacups. If your gift is stored in a mason jar, cover the lid with a round of paper or fabric and tie with a ribbon of raffia or twine. A small wooden crate, a tray, or a simple picnic basket are all good choices for holding larger items.

★ Joni's Favorites ★

A quality pepper mill is handy to have since fresh ground pepper is so much tastier than purchased ground pepper. Most convenient of all is the Pepper Gun which can be used with just one hand and is made by Tom David, Inc. Go to Peppergun.com on the Internet or call (800) 634-8881.

If you want the gift to be even more elaborate, present a batch of cookies in a cookie jar, or a cake on a covered cake plate. A friend of mine made pillows with cookie pockets sewn on the front and a delicious cookie tucked inside.

When you tie on the bow and tag, tuck a seasonal sprig, a bunch of grapes, a candy cane, or a silk flower into the ribbon to make your gift even more thoughtful. How about a bunch of baby carrots tied to a basket of carrot muffins? Or a wooden spoon tied to a package of dry pasta?

Tags and Instructions

Take time to make a clever tag and give your dish a fun name, if you like. "Heard You Were in a Jam" [or a "Pickle"], "I Relish Your Friendship," "From Your Nutty Neighbor," "To Spice Up Your Life," "Warm Thoughts of You," "Sweets for a Sweetie," "Instant De-Stresser," and other labels can make the gift extra special.

Cut the edges of the tag with fancy-edging scissors, or use some speckled card stock and your best lettering. Punch a hole in the tag, then tie on with ribbon. How about using old

photos for tags, available at thrift shops for just pennies? A large, smooth leaf with your friend's name written on it in gold ink is another clever tag. If your friend is going away, how about a luggage tag?

If your dish requires instructions (how to mix and bake the dough, for example), attach a recipe card with clear directions. Also let the recipient know if the product needs to be chilled. Sometimes it's thoughtful to include the recipe, or the history of the dish if it has one.

All of these little touches are sure to make your gift even more appreciated. But simply giving of yourself is the greatest gift of all, and taking the time to make something for others is the best way to let them know you really care.

Part Five

The Recipes

Chapter Sixteen

Breads, Cereals, Soups & Salads

✳ **1** promise the recipes in the following chapters are all easy! They have very few ingredients and very few steps. Many use convenience foods, such as frozen bread dough, a cake mix, or bottled minced ginger. And if you make more than you need, most can be frozen (though it's always nice to send guests home with a goodie box).

Breads, Cereals, Pasta

EASY STICKY RING

  1 loaf frozen bread dough, thawed
  1 cup pecan halves (optional)
  1 (3.5 oz.) package *not* instant butterscotch pudding
  ¾ cup brown sugar   *(recipe continues)*

1 teaspoon cinnamon
½ cup butter, melted

Butter a bundt pan and place pecans in bottom, rounded sides down. Cut or slice bread dough into bite-sized pieces and place atop pecans. In a small bowl, whisk pudding mix, sugar, and cinnamon, and sprinkle over dough. Next, drizzle on butter. Cover with plastic and chill overnight. The next morning, place pan in cold oven. Bake at 375 degrees for 30 minutes. Invert onto platter.

Makes 12 servings.

CHEDDAR & HERB BISCUITS

2 cups flour
1 tablespoon baking powder
¼ teaspoon salt

1 cup shredded cheddar cheese
½ cup freshly grated Parmesan cheese
1 tablespoon dried basil
1 teaspoon summer savory
1¼ cups whipping cream

Stir together flour, baking powder, salt, cheeses, and herbs. Add cream and stir until mixture forms a ball of dough. Knead briefly on a floured surface and roll out ½-inch thick. Cut into 2- or 3-inch rounds and place on an ungreased baking sheet. Bake at 425 degrees for 15 minutes or until golden, then cool on a rack.

Makes 12 servings.

> **Tip**
>
> **When rolling out and cutting pastry, always gather up the scraps and reroll them until all the dough is used. If you don't have a round cutter, use the rim of a glass, dipped in flour.**

ORANGE ROLLS

These almost function as currency in our house. And what an easy recipe!

2 cans refrigerated biscuits
½ cup (1 stick) butter
¾ cup sugar
Grated rind of 1 orange

Unwrap and separate biscuits. In a small saucepan, stir butter, sugar, and orange rind over medium heat until foamy. Dip biscuits halfway into mixture and arrange vertically inside a bundt pan. Pour any remaining drippings over tops of rolls. Bake on bottom rack at 400 degrees for 10–15 minutes. Invert on serving plate. Scrape any bits of orange sauce left in the pan onto the rolls.

Serves 1 teenage boy. Or 10 to 12 adults

HOMEMADE GRANOLA

This doubles well if you want to make a big batch to keep on hand—it will keep for 10 months in an airtight container. And it makes a great take-home gift for guests.

5 cups oatmeal
1½ cups chopped nuts
1 cup raw sunflower seeds
1 cup raisins, dried cranberries, or other dried fruit (optional)
1 cup coconut
½ cup sesame seeds
½ cup wheat germ
¾ cup brown sugar
¾ cup water
¾ cup vegetable oil
¼ cup honey
¼ cup molasses
½ teaspoon salt
1½ teaspoons cinnamon
2 teaspoons vanilla

In a large bowl, mix dry ingredients: oatmeal, nuts, seeds, raisins, coconut, wheat germ. Stir remaining ingredients in a saucepan over medium heat just until sugar dissolves (do not boil). Pour hot mixture over dry ingredients and mix thoroughly. Spread onto two baking sheets and bake 90 minutes at 200 degrees, stirring every 30 minutes.

Makes 10 cups.

BREAKFAST CASSEROLE

Make this the night before (let it become an easy Christmas morning tradition).

½ cup (1 stick) butter
6 slices sourdough bread
2 cups cooked, diced ham
3 cups shredded Swiss cheese
6 eggs
2 cups milk

Melt butter. Trim crusts from bread and dip slices into butter. Place on bottom of nine-by-thirteen-inch baking pan. Sprinkle ham, then cheese, over slices. Whisk eggs with milk and pour over all. Cover with foil and chill overnight. The next morning, bake uncovered for 45 minutes at 350 degrees.

Makes 8 to 12 servings.

CINNAMON-APPLE OVEN PANCAKES

(Or you may substitute any fresh seasonal fruit.)

Pancakes
3 eggs
½ teaspoon salt
½ cup flour
½ cup milk
2 tablespoons butter
Powdered sugar for dusting

Apple Topping
4 Granny Smith apples
4 tablespoons butter

(recipe continues)

⅔ cup brown sugar

½ teaspoon cinnamon

Heat two round cake pans in a 450-degree oven. In a small bowl, beat eggs and salt for 1 minute at high speed. Reduce speed to low and add flour and milk. Place 1 tablespoon butter in each cake pan and brush to coat pan. Pour batter into pans and return to oven for 15 minutes.

While pancakes bake, prepare topping. Peel and slice apples; combine with butter, sugar, and cinnamon in a medium saucepan over medium heat. Stir for 10 minutes; apples will soften and glaze will form.

When pancake has baked for 15 minutes, reduce oven heat to 350 degrees and bake another 5 minutes. Remove to serving plates, spoon apple topping onto each pancake, and dust with powdered sugar. Cut into wedges and serve.

Serves 4.

FRENCH BREAD ROLLS

2¼ cups warm water

2 packages yeast

2 tablespoons sugar

2 teaspoons salt

4–6 cups flour

Pour yeast and sugar into warm water and let set for 1 minute. Now mix well with salt and flour. Let rise 1 hour, punch down, then let rise another 30 minutes. Place golf-ball-sized pieces on greased baking sheet and let rise another 30 minutes. Bake at 400 degrees until brown, 20–30 minutes, depending on size of rolls.

PUMPKIN BREAD

This makes two loaves; give one to a neighbor, or freeze one for later.

1⅓ cups oil

5 eggs

2 cups solid-pack pumpkin

2 cups flour

2 cups sugar

2 (3 oz.) packages vanilla or coconut pie filling—*not* instant

1 teaspoon salt

1 teaspoon cinnamon

1 teaspoon nutmeg

1 teaspoon baking soda

1 cup nuts (optional)

Preheat oven to 350 degrees. In a large bowl, beat oil, eggs, and pumpkin. In another bowl, combine dry ingredients, then fold into pumpkin mixture. Beat well. Stir in nuts. Pour into two well-greased nine-by-five-inch loaf pans. Bake for 1 hour.

HOMEMADE WHITE BREAD

This recipe makes 2 loaves.

2 packages active dry yeast
¾ cup warm water
¼ cup sugar
2⅔ cups warm water
3 tablespoons shortening
1 tablespoon salt
9–10 cups flour
Nonstick cooking spray
Melted butter, approximately 2 tablespoons

Dissolve yeast in ¾ cup warm water, adding half the sugar. While yeast foams, place remaining warm water, sugar, shortening, salt, and half the flour in a large bowl. Add yeast mixture and beat until smooth. Add additional flour until dough is no longer sticky. Turn dough onto lightly floured surface and knead for 10 minutes. Spray a clean bowl with nonstick spray and place dough in bowl. Spray top of dough; cover and let rise in a warm place for 1 hour, or until double in bulk. Punch down, and divide in half. Form each half into a loaf and place in a greased nine-by-five-inch loaf pan. Brush with butter and let rise again for 1 hour. Bake on a low rack at 425 degrees for 30–35 minutes. Brush again with butter. Cool on wire rack.

CINNAMON ROLLS

Everyone should know how to make these. And, the dough makes wonderful dinner rolls.

Dough

2 packages yeast

½ cup warm water

1 tablespoon sugar

1 cup warm milk

2 eggs, beaten

¼ cup sugar

1 teaspoon salt

½ cup cooking oil

4–5 cups flour

Filling

1 cup brown sugar

½ cup sugar

½ cup (1 stick) butter, melted

1 cup raisins (optional)

1 cup chopped pecans (optional)

¼ cup cinnamon

Frosting

1 box powdered sugar

½ cup cream (thin with additional cream if necessary)

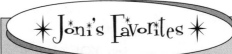

✳ Joni's Favorites ✳

Even if you never make pastry, you'll use Graham Kerr's stainless steel pastry cutter to cut a zillion other items. It's useful as a cleaver for slicing right through everything from sandwiches to steaks, and it scrapes dough off your cutting board, slices cinnamon rolls cleanly, and takes up little space.

In a small bowl or mug, mix yeast with warm water and 1 tablespoon sugar; set aside. In large bowl, mix warm milk, eggs, sugar, salt, and oil. Add yeast mixture when foamy; mix well. Add flour; knead well. Cover and let rise 30 minutes, or until double in bulk. Roll dough out on floured surface. Spread with mixture of all filling ingredients; adjust amounts to suit your taste. Roll dough up and slice into 1-inch-thick segments. Place rolls on greased baking sheet, cover, and let rise another 30 minutes. Bake for 10–12 minutes at 400 degrees. Remove from baking sheet. Combine frosting ingredients and drizzle over rolls.

Makes about 2 dozen.

YORKSHIRE PUDDINGS

These English popover rolls are not dessert puddings but a delicious bread side dish to serve with roast beef and gravy. (Yes, they are eaten with gravy.) Sometimes they're made in one large pan, but I like individual ones made in muffin tins.

2 eggs
1 cup milk
1 scant cup flour
1 pinch salt
Beef drippings from roast (⅓ cup)

While roast cools, raise oven temperature to 450 degrees. Beat eggs until fluffy, gradually adding flour and milk. Add salt and 2 tablespoons of the beef drippings. Place another tablespoon of the drippings into each muffin cup; place tin in oven until drippings sizzle. Remove tin and drop a large spoonful of batter into each hole. Cook for 10 minutes, then reduce heat to 350 degrees and cook 10–15 minutes more, until puddings are puffy and golden. Serve with roast beef and gravy.

Makes 12 servings.

PASTA WITH TOMATO-BASIL SAUCE

Boil the pasta 10 minutes before the sauce is done. This sauce is even better the next day.

2 tablespoons olive oil

½ onion, chopped

1 clove garlic, minced

2 (15 oz.) cans Italian tomatoes with basil

¼ lb. prosciutto ham, chopped

2 tablespoons dried basil

2 tablespoons grated Romano cheese

2 bay leaves

2 teaspoons chopped parsley

6–8 fennel seeds

1 teaspoon sugar

½ teaspoon salt

¼ teaspoon oregano

16 oz. package spinach pasta, cooked

In large saucepan, sauté onion and garlic in oil until onion is transparent. Add remaining ingredients. Bring to boil, then reduce heat and simmer ½ hour. Remove bay leaves. Pour over cooked pasta.

Makes 2 cups—can be poured over pasta for 6 to 8 servings.

MACARONI AND CHEESE

Everybody should know how to make this from scratch; it's a great comfort food and usually tops kids' lists of favorites.

2 cups large elbow macaroni

3 quarts boiling water

½ teaspoon onion salt *(recipe continues)*

½ teaspoon pepper

3 tablespoons butter

2 tablespoons flour

1 cup milk

3 cups shredded cheddar cheese (try this with Gruyère—yum!)

Pour macaroni into boiling water, cook until al dente. While pasta cooks, prepare sauce: In a small saucepan over medium heat, whisk salt, pepper, butter, and flour to form a smooth paste. Add milk, stirring until thickened but not boiling.

Drain pasta and pour half into a 2-quart casserole. Sprinkle with half the cheese, then the remaining half of the pasta. Add last half of cheese, then pour sauce over all. Cover and bake at 350 degrees for 30 minutes. Remove cover and bake for an additional 15 minutes.

Makes about 12 servings.

CREAMY POLENTA

Try this side dish instead of rice or potatoes for a refreshing change of pace.

4½ cups chicken stock or broth

1½ cups polenta

¾ teaspoon salt

4 tablespoons butter

½ cup freshly grated Parmesan cheese

¾ cup whipping cream

Bring broth to a boil in a medium saucepan over medium heat. Slowly whisk in polenta, then cover and simmer for 20 minutes. Stir in remaining ingredients and serve.

Makes 4 to 6 servings.

BASIC WHITE RICE

Boil twice as much water as the amount of uncooked rice you are adding—4 cups of water for 2 cups of uncooked rice. Then stir in the rice, cover the pot, and reduce the heat to low. Let rice cook for 15 minutes, then remove it from the heat and let it set another 5 minutes.

CHILI RICE

This is a great side dish for supper.

>   4 cups cooked rice
>   2 cups sour cream
>   1–2 (4.5 oz.) cans chopped mild green chilies
>   3 cups shredded Monterey Jack cheese
>   1 cup shredded cheddar cheese

In a large bowl, mix all ingredients except cheddar cheese. Turn into a greased baking dish and bake at 350 degrees for 15 minutes. During last five minutes of baking, sprinkle with cheddar cheese.
   Makes 6 to 8 servings.

Soups & Salads

CHEESEBURGER SOUP

>   1 lb. ground beef
>   ½ cup chopped onion
>   ½ cup chopped celery
>   3 tablespoons flour

(recipe continues)

4 cups milk
1 tablespoon beef bouillon granules
1 cup shredded cheddar cheese

Stir beef, celery, and onion in a skillet over medium heat until beef is crumbly. Pour off drippings. Stir in flour. Add milk and bouillon, stirring until thick. Turn off heat and stir in cheese. Serve when cheese melts.

Makes 4 to 6 servings.

CRAB BISQUE

Best if made a day ahead and then reheated when you need it, this is a good one when you're entertaining.

¼ cup butter
½ cup chopped onion
½ cup chopped celery
2 tablespoons flour
½ teaspoon salt
6 drops Tabasco sauce
1 cup chicken broth
2 cups half & half
½ lb. lump crab meat
Fresh dill, chopped

Melt butter in a large skillet and sauté onion and celery until onion is transparent. Stir in flour, salt, Tabasco. Increase temperature to medium. Slowly add broth and bring to a boil.

Transfer liquid to blender and blend smooth. Pour back into skillet. Adjust heat to lowest setting. Add half & half and crab, stirring until thickened (about 10 minutes). If making a day ahead, reheat carefully over a low setting or in the top of a double boiler. Garnish with fresh chopped dill.

Makes 4 to 6 servings.

CLAM CHOWDER

½ cup (1 stick) butter, plus 2 tablespoons
½ cup flour
4 small new potatoes, diced
½ cup onion, chopped
1 cup celery, chopped
½ cup flour
1½ quarts half & half
2 (6 oz.) cans minced clams, with juice
Freshly ground pepper

In a large skillet, sauté potatoes, onion, and celery in 2 tablespoons of the butter until fork-tender. Meanwhile, melt ½ cup butter in a soup pot and stir in flour to form a smooth paste. Slowly stir in half & half to make a white sauce. Add sautéed potato mixture, clams, and ground pepper to sauce mixture. Add milk to thin, if necessary. Simmer, but do not boil.

Makes 8 to 10 servings.

PUMPKIN SOUP

3 tablespoons butter
1 onion, chopped
1 cup finely chopped celery
2 (15 oz.) cans chicken broth
2 cups canned solid pumpkin
1 tablespoon curry powder
1 teaspoon thyme
1 cup cream
Salt and pepper to taste   *(recipe continues)*

In a large soup pot, sauté onion and celery in butter until tender. Add remaining ingredients, stirring just until heated through.

Makes 6 servings.

SIMPLE CHICKEN SALAD

    4 cups cooked chicken
    2 cups celery, diced
    3 hard-cooked eggs, sliced
    1 medium-sized bottle stuffed green olives, sliced
    4 green onions, chopped (including tops)
    1 cup crushed pecans or walnuts
    Mayonnaise to moisten
    2 tablespoons lemon juice

Mix all ingredients and chill.

Makes 4 to 6 servings.

RASPBERRY-CRANBERRY JELL-O

Bring this for Christmas or Thanksgiving—it's a crimson-and-white-striped Jell-O salad, easy but scrumptious (and it doubles well for a crowd).

    1 (6 oz.) package cherry Jell-O
    1 cup boiling water
    1 can whole cranberry sauce
    1 (10 oz.) package frozen raspberries
    1 (20 oz.) can crushed pineapple with juice
    1 cup sour cream

Dissolve gelatin in water. In a large bowl, mix dissolved gelatine with cranberry sauce, raspberries, and crushed pineapple. Pour half of mixture into 8-inch-square dish. Chill. Spread sour cream over chilled mixture. Add remaining half of gelatin mixture. Chill. Cut into squares and serve on a lettuce leaf.

Makes 9 servings.

POTATO SALAD

I wonder if marriages have broken up over the right way to make potato salad. Some like it with dill, some with onion, others with vinegar. It seems everyone feels passionate about her mom's being the best, so here's my mom's:

> 2 lbs. (6 medium) potatoes
> 1 cup mayonnaise
> ½ cup milk
> ⅓ cup pickle relish
> 1 tablespoon whole-grain mustard
> 1 teaspoon onion powder
> ½ teaspoon black pepper
> 4 hard-cooked eggs, peeled and diced
> Paprika for garnish

Boil potatoes for 20–25 minutes, or until fork-tender. Peel and cube. In a large bowl, combine all remaining ingredients, then fold in diced potatoes. Add additional milk if necessary. Sprinkle with paprika and chill.

Makes 6 to 8 servings.

> ✴ Joni's Favorites ✴
>
> **A skinny scraper is one of the most-used items in our kitchen. It's perfect for reaching into narrow-necked bottles, or for quickly spreading mayonnaise on a row of assembly-line sandwiches. It's just right for frosting cakes, too.**

FAJITA SALAD

> ½ lb. top sirloin steak, cut ¾-inch thick
> 1 tablespoon lime juice
> 2 teaspoons cooking oil

(recipe continues)

4 drops Tabasco sauce

1 red or yellow bell pepper

1 green bell pepper

½ onion

1 package mixed salad greens

2 cups shredded cheese—a mixture of cheddar and jack

Cut steak into strips. Marinate in lime juice, oil, and Tabasco sauce in the refrigerator for 30 minutes.

Meanwhile, slice peppers and onions into strips and place in large skillet. Add meat mixture and stir-fry over high heat until vegetables are crisp-tender and meat is no longer pink.

Serve hot over mixed greens. Top with cheese.

Makes 4 servings.

PESTO RICE SALAD

4 cups cooked white rice

1 cup bottled roasted red peppers, chopped

1 cup sliced black olives

½ cup prepared pesto sauce

½ cup pine nuts

Use an egg slicer to cut mushrooms and olives.

Mix all ingredients and chill. Serve on lettuce leaves, or with a medley of other chilled salads.

Makes 4 to 6 servings.

TROPICAL SET SALAD

This is the yummiest gelatin salad you've ever tasted (it's the topping that makes it so good).

Salad

1 (6 oz.) box orange gelatin
2 cups boiling water
1 (16 oz.) can crushed pineapple, with juice
2 bananas cut into small chunks

Topping

1 cup sugar
2 tablespoons flour
1 egg, beaten
1 cup apricot nectar
1 cup whipping cream, whipped (or 2 cups whipped cream)
1 cup shredded cheddar cheese

Stir gelatin into boiling water. Add pineapple (with juice) and bananas. Pour into a nine-by-thirteen-inch pan and chill until firm. To make topping, stir sugar, flour, egg, and nectar in a small saucepan over medium heat. Cook until it coats a spoon, pudding consistency. Set aside to cool. Fold in whipping cream and spread topping over gelatin. Sprinkle with cheese.

Makes 12 to 15 servings.

DEVILED EGGS

Try adding your own variation—use Thousand Island dressing instead of mayonnaise, or add a pinch of curry, minced onion, or a scoop of chopped olives.

6 hard-cooked eggs, peeled
¼ cup mayonnaise
1 tablespoon pickle relish
1 teaspoon whole-grain mustard
Pinch of pepper
Paprika for garnish

Slice eggs in half lengthwise. Scoop yolks into a small bowl. Use a fork to mash with with mayonnaise, relish, mustard, and pepper. Spoon or pipe yolk mixture back into egg halves; sprinkle with paprika. Keep chilled.

Makes 12 halves.

Chapter Seventeen

The Main Course

Meats & Main Dishes

STREAMLINED BEEF STROGANOFF

This dish is superb for family or company, and doubles well for a larger gathering, too.

    1 lb. top sirloin steak, cut into cubes or strips
    2 tablespoons Worcestershire sauce
    1 tablespoon lemon juice
    ½ teaspoon black pepper
    2 tablespoons cooking oil
    1 lb. mushrooms, sliced (use portobellos for extra flavor)
    1 large onion, thinly sliced
    1 (15 oz.) can beef broth
    2 tablespoons flour
    1 cup sour cream (may use low-fat)
    1½ teaspoons paprika

Place beef, Worcestershire sauce, juice, and pepper in a large, resealable bag; toss to coat. Marinate in refrigerator 2 hours.

Heat oil in large skillet over medium heat. Sauté onion until lightly browned, about 5 minutes. Add mushrooms and sauté for 2 minutes. Transfer to a bowl and keep warm.

In same skillet, brown beef over high heat for 2 minutes. In a small bowl, whisk together broth and flour, and add to beef along with onions and mushrooms. Boil until sauce is thick enough to coat a spoon, about 2 minutes. Reduce heat to low. Stir in sour cream and paprika, but do not let Stroganoff boil; just stir until heated through. Serve over pasta.

Makes 4 to 6 servings.

LUNCHMEAT ROLL-UP SANDWICHES

These are great for a picnic or tailgate party, or pack them in your lunch. Great to make ahead of time and chill, even overnight.

> 2 (10-inch) flour tortillas
> 6 oz. soft garden herb cheese spread (or other flavors)
> 1 lb. deli meat, thinly sliced (ham, chicken, beef, or a mix)
> ¾ cup finely grated Monterey Jack cheese
> 1 cup shredded lettuce

Spread tortillas with soft cheese spread, then layer on remaining ingredients. Roll up and wrap tightly with plastic; chill. Serve sliced in pinwheel segments, or cut each "log" in two and eat burrito-style.

Makes 4 servings.

This is an easy recipe to tinker with; some other ingredients to try include sliced olives, relish, chopped celery, salsa, cilantro, feta cheese, tuna, roasted red peppers, nuts, cabbage—just about anything you could put in a wrap.

BARBECUED CHICKEN PIZZA

This is so easy—you'll love it!

> 2 cups diced, cooked chicken
> ½ cup bottled barbecue sauce
> 1 prepared pizza crust (such as Boboli)
> ½ red onion, sliced
> 2 tablespoons fresh cilantro, chopped
> 2 cups shredded mozzarella cheese

In a large bowl, stir diced chicken with barbecue sauce. Spread over pizza crust. Sprinkle with red onion and cilantro; cover with mozzarella. Bake at 400 degrees until cheese is bubbly, about 10 minutes.

MACADAMIA-CRUSTED SALMON

> 1 cup macadamia nuts
> 4 salmon fillets, 1 inch thick
> 2 eggs, beaten
> 1 teaspoon freshly grated ginger
> ⅓ cup coconut syrup or coconut milk

Preheat oven to 350 degrees. Whirl macadamia nuts in blender or food processor to finely crush. Stir ginger into eggs. Dip salmon fillets into egg mixture, then into nuts to coat. Place in greased baking dish and drizzle lightly with coconut syrup. Bake 15 minutes, or until opaque.

Makes 4 servings.

LAMB SHANKS

½ cup freshly grated Parmesan cheese
½ cup Italian-flavored bread crumbs
1 teaspoon red pepper flakes
4 lamb shanks (about 1 lb. each)
½ cup apricot jam
2 tablespoons olive oil
½ cup orange juice

In a small bowl, combine Parmesan cheese, bread crumbs, and red pepper flakes. Set aside. Cover all sides of shanks with apricot jam. Dip shanks into crumb mixture to coat thoroughly. Brown in oil in a large skillet or Dutch oven over medium heat. Pour orange juice around, but not onto, shanks. Cover, reduce heat, and simmer 2½ hours or until tender.

Makes 4 servings.

SPICY STEAK

1½ lbs. boneless beef top sirloin steak, about 1¼ inches thick
⅓ cup prepared mustard
½ cup bread crumbs
1 teaspoon chili powder
½ teaspoon garlic powder

Spread steak on both sides with mustard. In a small bowl, combine bread crumbs, chili powder, and garlic powder. Press onto both sides of steak. Broil 3 to 4 inches from heat for 15–20 minutes. Slice crosswise to serve.

Makes 6 servings.

QUICHE WITH AVOCADO/TOMATO SALSA

This easy quiche makes its own crust. It's terrific for breakfast, brunch, or a light dinner.

3 eggs
1½ cups milk
½ cup buttermilk baking mix
¼ cup melted butter
4 drops Tabasco sauce
1 cup cooked meat (bacon, sausage, etc.) or vegetables
   (broccoli, peppers, spinach, asparagus, corn, carrots,
   you name it)
1 cup shredded cheddar cheese
1 avocado, diced
1 tomato, diced (or substitute mango)
1 tablespoon cilantro, chopped
1 teaspoon lemon juice

Preheat oven to 350 degrees. In a blender or food processor, whirl first five ingredients. Place meat or vegetables and cheddar cheese in a greased 9-inch baking dish. Pour blended mixture over all. Bake 40 minutes; let cool 10 minutes before slicing. Top with a mixture of avocado, tomato, cilantro, and lemon juice.

CHICKEN PIZZA ROULADE

A roulade is simply a rolled-up anything—cake, roast, etc. It's a showy dish because each slice reveals a colorful pinwheel design.

6 boneless, skinless, split chicken breasts
1 (15 oz.) can pizza sauce
2 cups bread crumbs
2 cups shredded mozzarella cheese   *(recipe continues)*

Preheat oven to 350 degrees. Place chicken breasts between two sheets of plastic wrap or waxed paper, and pound until ¼ inch thick. Mix pizza sauce with bread crumbs and spread over chicken. Sprinkle with mozzarella cheese. Roll up each breast and secure with wooden picks. Salt and pepper roulades. Spray baking pan with nonstick oil, then place chicken in pan and bake for 45 minutes. Slice and arrange on platter before serving.

Makes 6 servings.

SWEET & SPICY SCALLOPS

    1 (8 oz.) carton Key lime pie-flavored yogurt
    2 tablespoons whole-grain mustard
    1 tablespoon lime juice
    2 teaspoons minced canned chipotle chilies
    1 teaspoon minced garlic
    16 large sea scallops
    3 tablespoons cooking oil
    4 cups cooked rice

In a large bowl, combine yogurt, mustard, lime juice, chilies, and garlic. Marinate scallops in this mixture in refrigerator for 30 minutes or more. Heat oil in skillet over medium heat. Pour scallops and marinade into skillet. Cook until scallops are opaque, about 5 minutes. Serve over warm rice.

Makes 4 servings.

ROAST LAMB

    1 cup honey-mustard salad dressing
    2 tablespoons chopped fresh thyme

2 tablespoons chopped fresh tarragon

1 teaspoon crushed garlic

6-lb. lamb boneless shoulder

Whisk first four ingredients to make a marinade. Refrigerate lamb in this mixture overnight. (Make sure all sides of meat are coated.) Roast lamb the following day, fat side up, covered, at 325 degrees for 2 hours.

Makes 12 servings.

A cast-iron Dutch oven is great for browning meat, letting foods stew, and cooking a million other things. It's heavy and you do have to wash, dry, and oil it—but it's worth it.

"BARBECUED" CHICKEN

2 tablespoons cooking oil

3–4 lbs. chicken pieces

½ cup chopped onion

¾ cup ketchup

⅓ cup vinegar

3 tablespoons brown sugar

2 teaspoons prepared mustard

1 tablespoon Worcestershire sauce

Salt and pepper to taste

In a large skillet, brown chicken pieces in oil, then remove with tongs and place in nine-by-thirteen-inch baking dish. Place chicken in a 350-degree oven for 1 hour. While chicken is baking, sauté onion in same skillet, until transparent. Add remaining ingredients and simmer 10 minutes. Baste chicken with this mixture as soon as mixture has simmered. Return chicken to oven to finish baking.

Makes 6 servings.

STEAK (INSERT YOUR NAME HERE)

Hey, if there can be Steak Diane, why can't there be Steak Jennifer? This will be your own creation, given unique flavors based upon whichever spice rub you choose.

> 4 beef eye round or tenderloin steaks, cut 1 inch thick
> Garlic-flavored cooking spray
> 4 tablespoons prepared spice rub (there are so many to choose from: Jamaican, East Indian, Asian, Cuban, Southern, Provençale, Tex-Mex, etc.)

Spray both sides of steaks with garlic cooking spray, to help spices adhere. Press spices into meat. Heat a heavy skillet over medium heat. Fry steaks 5 minutes per side—how easy is that! (Be sure to slice across the grain for tender-tasting meat.) This steak (and just about any fish or chicken) is wonderful with the following sauce if you want to whip up a creamy complement to the spiced steaks while they're cooking.

BOB'S 1-2-3 SAUCE

My husband created this scrumptious sauce, which has a very easy formula:

> 1 part mayonnaise
> 2 parts whole-grain mustard
> 3 parts sour cream

Stir in a small saucepan over low heat just until heated through. Pour over steak, chicken, or fish.

ENGLISH FISH 'N' CHIPS

My "veddy English" paternal grandmother was so well known for her fish 'n' chips that she taught restaurant chefs how to make this typically British dish. Here's her recipe:

2 lbs. halibut, boned and skinned (or prepared fillets)

¾ cup flour

1 teaspoon baking powder

Enough water to make thick paste

2 cups shortening, or enough to measure 4–5 inches deep
     when melted; oil can be substituted

4 large potatoes

Fish   Cut fish into three-by-three-inch pieces. Mix flour, baking powder, and water into a thick paste and coat fish pieces with this batter.

Heat shortening or oil until blue-hot (375 degrees). You want the oil hot, but not smoking. Fry fish in oil until brown and crispy on both sides—about 4–5 minutes.

Chips   Wash and peel potatoes, then cut into lengthwise strips of desired thickness (English chips are much thicker than french fries). These are cooked in the same oil as the fish and do not absorb the fish flavor. Remove when chips are brown and can be pierced with a fork.

Makes 6 servings.

(Be sure to serve the fish with malt vinegar!)

ROAST CHICKEN

Everyone should know how to roast a chicken, and here's an easy way to prepare this basic dish.

1 whole chicken (about 3½ lbs.)

3 tablespoons butter

Herbs and seasonings of your choice

Salt and pepper to taste

Remove giblets and neck from cavity of chicken. Rinse chicken inside and out; pat dry with paper towels. Cut fat from cavity opening, tuck wing tips under chicken (if they won't stay, cover tips with foil to prevent burning). Tie legs together with kitchen twine. Insert seasonings under skin or loosely inside chicken. Place breast-side-up on a rack in roasting pan. Rub chicken with butter. Salt and pepper, if desired. Bake uncovered at 450 degrees for 1 hour. Chicken is done when juices run clear if pierced with a knife, or when thermometer inserted in thickest part of thigh reads 175 degrees. Let stand 10 minutes before cutting string and carving.

Makes 4 servings.

Variations:

* Tuck sage, basil, rosemary, or thyme leaves under skin; 3 or 4 sprigs in cavity.
* Surround chicken with vegetables, especially onion chunks.
* Rub prepared, purchased spice mixture under skin—try Asian, East Indian, Mexican, Cajun, Mediterranean, Cuban—you name it.
* Instead of rubbing chicken with butter, try a seasoned oil, such as sesame oil.

* Place bay leaves under the skin—arrange to look like actual growing leaves.
* Cover chicken with a melted fruit jelly.
* Insert grated orange or lemon peel under the skin.
* Roast cloves of garlic around the chicken; tuck a few inside.

SHRIMP ON ROSEMARY SKEWERS

24 large raw shrimp
½ cup honey-mustard salad dressing
4 (8 inch) rosemary sprigs

Peel shrimp, but leave tails on. Place in bowl with dressing; toss to coat. Strip skewers clean (just pull down the skewer with your hand and the needles will pop off). Thread shrimp onto skewers, then place on oiled broiler pan and broil 3 minutes per side. (Make shish kebabs by alternating shrimp with vegetables, or with another meat.)

Makes 4 servings.

HARVEST FRITTATA

This makes a wonderful brunch dish or dinner entrée. If you have a cast-iron skillet, use it for this.

3 tablespoons olive oil

1 cup red pepper, diced

1 cup yellow crook-necked squash, diced

2 green onions, chopped

1½ cups cooked ham (or turkey or crab), diced

1 teaspoon chopped fresh basil

6 eggs, beaten

½ cup shredded Romano or Parmesan cheese

3 tablespoons chopped parsley

✳ Joni's Favorites ✳

I have a wonderful set of T-Fal pans with handles that snap off so they can be stacked like mixing bowls, if space is a consideration. I also like my Chantal cookware with clear glass lids that let me see what's cooking.

In a large, ovenproof skillet, heat oil and sauté pepper, squash, and onions until fork-tender. Add ham and basil; pour eggs over all. Cook like an omelette, lifting cooked sections with a spatula to allow uncooked egg to flow beneath. When frittata is set and edges are beginning to tan, sprinkle with Parmesan and slip under broiler to brown top slightly, just a minute or two. Remove from oven, sprinkle with parsley, cut into wedges.

Makes 4 to 6 servings.

MEXICAN CASSEROLE

1½ lbs. ground beef
½ onion, chopped
1 package taco seasoning mix
1 cup water
1 dozen corn tortillas
1 large can enchilada sauce
3 cups shredded cheddar cheese

In a large skillet over medium heat, brown beef and onion until beef is crumbly. Add seasoning mix and water; simmer 10 minutes. In a buttered nine-by-thirteen-inch casserole dish, layer tortillas, enchilada sauce, taco meat, and cheese. Repeat several times, ending with cheese. Bake uncovered at 350 degrees for 30 minutes.

Fruit & Vegetable Side Dishes

COWBOY BEANS 'N' BACON

4 strips bacon, fried and diced (you can purchase already cooked bacon, then just cut it up with shears)
1 onion, chopped (or use frozen chopped onion)
1 (16 oz.) can kidney beans, drained
1 (16 oz.) can whole tomatoes with liquid, chopped
1 (15 oz.) can pinto beans, drained
1 (15 oz.) can beef broth
2 tablespoons ketchup
1 teaspoon garlic powder

¾ teaspoon chili powder

½ teaspoon ground cumin

¼ teaspoon red pepper flakes

1 bay leaf

In a large stew pot, fry bacon, drain on paper towels, dice with shears, and return bacon to pot. Sauté onion in bacon drippings, or if using already cooked bacon, sauté onion in 2 tablespoons vegetable oil. Add all other ingredients and simmer 10 minutes before serving. Remember to remove the bay leaf before serving.

Makes 8 to 10 servings.

HOT ARTICHOKE DIP

2 (14 oz.) cans artichoke hearts, drained and chopped

1 (4.5 oz.) can chopped mild green chilies

½ cup freshly grated Parmesan cheese

1 cup grated mozzarella cheese

1 cup mayonnaise

½ teaspoon garlic powder

Crackers

Mix all ingredients in a large bowl. Turn into a lightly greased (or sprayed) small casserole dish and bake at 350 degrees for 20 minutes. Serve with crackers.

Makes 6 to 8 servings.

CORN CASSEROLE

This is extremely easy and great for a crowd, as it doubles well. Kids love it.

1 (15 oz.) can whole kernel corn

1 (15 oz.) can creamed corn   *(recipe continues)*

½ cup (1 stick) butter, melted

1 cup sour cream

1 (8.5 oz.) package corn muffin mix, such as Jiffy

Combine all ingredients. Pour into a greased casserole dish. Bake at 350 degrees for 1 hour.

Makes 8 servings.

- -

EASY AU GRATIN POTATOES

4 lbs. potatoes (about 12 medium)

1 cup chopped onion (optional)

1 cup chopped, cooked bacon (optional)

Salt and pepper to taste

1½ cups whipping cream

1 cup shredded cheese, your choice

Wash, peel, and slice potatoes. Preheat oven to 425 degrees.

Layer potato slices, onion, and bacon in a buttered nine-by-thirteen-inch baking dish. Season to taste. In a small saucepan, bring cream to a boil, then reduce to simmer and stir in cheese until melted. Pour over potatoes. Cover with foil and bake for 1 hour.

Makes 8 to 10 servings.

- -

BAKED STUFFED TOMATOES

2 large tomatoes, halved

½ cup Italian-flavored bread crumbs

½ cup freshly grated Parmesan cheese

2 tablespoons fresh basil (or 1 tablespoon dried)

2 tablespoons melted butter

Scoop out inside of each tomato half and mix with bread crumbs, Parmesan, basil, salt, and pepper in a small bowl.

Place tomatoes, cut side up, in baking dish. Spoon mixture into each tomato half. Drizzle with melted butter. Bake at 350 degrees for 25 minutes.

Makes 4 servings.

PORTOBELLO MUSHROOMS STUFFED WITH SPINACH

These extra-large, extra-tasty mushrooms would make a terrific vegetarian main course, or a hearty side dish alongside a light piece of fish.

Garlic-flavored cooking spray
4 portobello mushrooms
1 (10 oz.) package frozen spinach, squeezed dry
½ cup ricotta cheese
2 tablespoons mayonnaise
2 teaspoons fresh chopped basil
1 teaspoon minced garlic
Salt and pepper to taste
4 ¼-inch-thick slices mozzarella cheese
Additional chopped basil for garnish

Spray a baking dish with cooking oil, and place mushrooms cap-side-down in dish. In a medium bowl, mix spinach, ricotta, mayonnaise, basil, garlic, salt, and pepper. Spoon into mushrooms. Cover each with a slice of cheese. Bake at 350 degrees for 20 minutes. Sprinkle with additional basil.

Makes 4 servings.

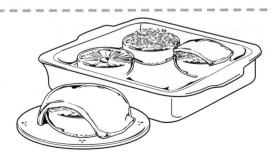

GUACAMOLE

This is one recipe you can tinker with, adding more or less of what you like.

3 medium avocados, peeled and pitted
1 tomato, diced
1 green onion, minced
1 tablespoon lime juice
1 tablespoon minced cilantro
8 drops Tabasco sauce
3 tablespoons mayonnaise

In a medium bowl, mash avocados with a fork. Stir in remaining ingredients. Serve with tortilla chips or as an accompaniment to any Mexican salad or main dish.

Makes 1½ cups.

BASIC WHITE SAUCE

This is an excellent sauce to serve with vegetables, of course, but it's also the basis of many meat sauces, soups, and gravies.

2 tablespoons butter
2 tablespoons flour
1 cup milk
Salt and pepper to taste

Melt butter over low heat in a small saucepan. Whisk in flour to make a smooth paste. Increase heat to medium, and slowly add milk and seasonings. The sauce will thicken as it comes to a boil.

Makes 1 cup.

VEGGIE TOSTADAS

2 tablespoons olive oil

1 cup onion, sliced

1 cup zucchini, sliced

1 cup roasted red peppers, sliced

1 cup mushrooms, sliced

1 (4.5 oz.) can chopped mild green chilies

8 crisp corn tortillas

1 tomato, chopped

1 cup shredded cheddar cheese

½ cup sour cream

1 avocado, chopped

Pine nuts are a great addition to many foods and can be frozen—as can all nuts—so you can just take out as many as you need and keep them fresh.

Preheat oven to 350 degrees. Heat oil in a large skillet over medium heat. Sauté onion, zucchini, red peppers, mushrooms, and green chilies until all are fork-tender. Place tortillas on baking sheet; top with vegetable mixture. Sprinkle with tomatoes and cheese. Bake for 5 minutes. Top with sour cream and chopped avocado.

Makes 8 servings.

HOLY STROMBOLI

You can make this a dynamite vegetarian dish by omitting the salami. Fool around with the ingredients; almost anything will work.

1 uncooked pizza dough crust (thaw a frozen one, unroll a canned one, or make one from scratch)

Garlic-flavored nonstick cooking spray

8 slices salami (optional)

2 cups shredded mozzarella cheese

(recipe continues)

1 cup sliced black olives
1 cup roasted red peppers, sliced
½ onion, minced
¼ cup freshly snipped basil
8–10 cloves peeled, roasted garlic (available in bottles)

This may sound odd, but consider buying a lemon tree and keeping it in a pot (they're very happy in confined containers) on your patio. Whenever you need a fresh splash of lemon juice, pluck one off the tree.

Preheat oven to 375 degrees. Roll out pizza dough on oil-sprayed baking sheet. Layer remaining ingredients lengthwise down center of dough, sprinkling on basil and tucking garlic in here and there. Fold up sides of dough over filling, and pinch to seal. Also pinch to seal ends. Spray with additional garlic-flavored oil. Bake 25 minutes. Slice and serve.

Makes 6 servings.

Chapter Eighteen

Dessert Recipes

BREAD PUDDING

This is a great way to use stale slices of bread, or leftover cinnamon rolls.
Try it with all kinds of breads.

Butter (4 oz. or ½ stick)

7 slices bread

½ cup raisins (optional—if you use them, soak them in hot
    water first to plump them up)

3 cups milk

(recipe continues)

⅔ cup sugar

4 eggs

1 teaspoon vanilla

½ teaspoon cinnamon

Remove crusts from bread, and butter one side of each slice. Place the slices, buttered side down, in an eight-by-eleven-inch baking dish. Be sure to line the sides as well as the bottom. In a large bowl, beat milk, sugar, eggs, vanilla, and cinnamon. Stir in raisins. Pour over bread.

Place dish in a larger pan on oven rack. Create water bath by filling larger pan with water until it reaches two-thirds the depth of the pudding dish. Bake at 350 degrees for 45 minutes, or until a knife inserted in the center comes out clean.

Great with whipped cream.

Some yummy additions to try: Crushed pecans, red-hot candies, chocolate chips, coconut, lemon zest, chopped dates.

Makes 8 servings.

STRAWBERRY CAKE

This basic recipe has been around for more than a century; I've updated it with the addition of strawberries and strawberry extract.

Cake

7 eggs

6 drops red food coloring

½ cup sugar

7 tablespoons cake flour

Pinch of salt

2 teaspoons strawberry extract (to make a plain cake, use 1 teaspoon vanilla in place of the strawberry extract)

Frosting and Filling

2 batches cream cheese frosting

2 cups diced strawberries

Additional whole or sliced berries for garnish

Preheat oven to 350 degrees. Separate eggs. Beat yolks with coloring, sugar, and flour until light and fluffy. In a separate bowl, beat egg whites until fairly stiff, then fold into yolk mixture with strawberry extract. Turn batter into two greased and floured cake pans. Bake for 20 minutes. Cool 5 minutes, then remove from pans. Cool completely; slice each cake in two horizontally, to create four layers.

Prepare a double batch of cream cheese frosting (p. 268). Into one batch, stir the diced strawberries and use them as filling between cake layers. Use remaining frosting to frost cake, then garnish with whole or sliced berries on top.

Makes 6 to 8 servings.

PEACH PIE

This is a must when peaches are in season! (Peel peaches easily by blanching them first—dip in boiling water for 30 seconds.)

Dough for two 9-inch pie crusts, rolled out

5 cups fresh sliced peaches (about 9 peaches)

Juice of 1 lemon

1 cup sugar

¼ cup flour

¼ teaspoon cinnamon

Dash of nutmeg

2 tablespoons butter

Preheat oven to 425 degrees. Place one pastry in 9-inch pie plate, reserving the other for a top crust. In a large bowl, mix peaches, lemon juice, sugar, flour, cinnamon, and nutmeg. Turn into crust. Dot with butter and cover with remaining crust. Pinch edges to seal. Cut slits in crust to vent. Bake for 35–40 minutes.

Makes 6 to 8 servings.

APPLE PIE

Make the same way as peach pie, but decrease the sugar by ¼ cup, increase the sliced apples by 1 cup, and use a whole teaspoon of cinnamon.

CAKE DECORATOR'S FROSTING

1¼ cups shortening
2 lbs. powdered sugar
½ cup water
1 teaspoon salt
1 teaspoon flavoring (vanilla, strawberry, etc.)

In a large bowl, cream shortening and sugar (add slowly) until fluffy. Add water a little at a time until mixture is smooth. Add salt and flavoring.

Makes enough frosting for 1 cake.

CINNAMON CRÈME BRÛLÉE

This easy, delicious custard with a caramelized sugar topping always brings compliments for the cook. (Just be sure to make them the day before.)

2 cups whipping cream
5 egg yolks
½ cup sugar
1 tablespoon vanilla

1 tablespoon cinnamon (or, omit cinnamon and make a
   plain brûlée)
½ cup brown sugar*

In a large bowl, whisk together cream, yolks, sugar, vanilla, and
cinnamon. Pour into 5 or 6 ramekins, or individual, ovenproof
baking dishes. Place ramekins in a nine-by-thirteen-inch baking
pan, and pour water into the pan until it comes halfway up the
sides of the ramekins (this is called a water bath, and will allow
the custards to bake slowly). Bake at 300 degrees for 45–60
minutes, or until custard edges are set (the middle will not be).
Cooking times will vary depending on the size of your ramekins. Now set pan of ramekins and water on a cooling rack for
10 minutes, then remove ramekins from water. Chill overnight.
When ready to serve, place ramekins on a baking sheet and
sprinkle each with brown sugar. Broil 5 inches from heat with
oven door open, until sugar caramelizes. (Chefs use a welding
torch.) Let stand 5 minutes, then serve. Ideally, the inside of
the custard will be cool and the crust warm.

   Makes 5 to 6 servings.

* 1–2 tablespoons of powdered sugar per ramekin may be substituted for brown sugar.

- -

NO-BAKE FUDGE

1 (3 oz.) package cream cheese, softened
1¼ lbs. butter, softened
1 lb. (1 box) powdered sugar
1 teaspoon vanilla
Nuts (optional)

In a large bowl, beat ingredients with electric mixer until thoroughly combined. Chill.

Makes 2½ cups.

- -

LEMON CURD FOR LEMON TARTLETS

This recipe is from my English nana, whose culinary skill is immortalized with every delicious bite! Curd is a thick, pudding-like filling for tarts. It also makes a delicious filling between cake layers, or a delightful topping for scones, toast, or cheesecake. I usually double the recipe for my large family.

2 eggs
½ cup (1 stick) butter
1 cup sugar
Juice of 2 lemons (about ⅓ cup)
Whipping cream, whipped
4 dozen tiny pie pastry tart shells (or use 2 dozen muffin-tin-sized shells)

Beat eggs and sugar in top of double boiler over simmering water until light and fluffy (3–5 minutes). Mix in juice and butter. Keep stirring until mixture thickens (20 minutes). Remove from heat and cool, then chill. Mixture will continue to thicken as it cools. Drop a spoonful of lemon curd into each tart shell; top with whipped cream. Curd can be stored in the refrigerator for a week. (For a more transparent curd, use 1 egg and 1 egg *yolk*.)

Makes 48 small tarts.

CHOCOLATE CRACKLE COOKIES

These soft, fudgy cookies will be white with chocolate crevices and cracks.

4 squares (4 oz.) unsweetened chocolate

½ cup cooking oil

2 cups sugar

4 eggs

2 teaspoons vanilla

2 cups flour

2 teaspoons baking powder

½ teaspoon salt

1 cup powdered sugar

In top of a double boiler, melt chocolate over simmering water. Blend in oil and sugar. Add eggs one at a time, beating after each. Add vanilla. Sift in the flour, baking powder, and salt. Chill dough several hours or overnight. Preheat oven to 350 degrees. Drop small portions of dough into powdered sugar and form into 1-inch balls. Place on greased baking sheet and bake for 10–12 minutes. *Do not overbake.*

Makes 5 to 6 dozen.

✳ Joni's Favorites ✳

If you don't want to make scones from scratch, Ivy Cottage is the best brand to buy, and currant is their best flavor. It's made by a company called Fremont Lane in Pasadena, California (626) 792-4850, but should be available in specialty stores and other markets. This makes a great hostess gift, too.

APPLE SQUARES

2 cups sugar

2 eggs

¾ cup vegetable oil

(recipe continues)

2 cups self-rising flour

2 teaspoons cinnamon

3 cups peeled, diced Granny Smith apples

1 cup chopped nuts

1 cup butterscotch chips

Preheat oven to 350 degrees. Grease a nine-by-thirteen-inch baking pan. In a large bowl, beat sugar, eggs, and oil. Add flour and cinnamon. Stir in apples and nuts. Sprinkle with chips. Bake 35–40 minutes. Cool completely before slicing.

Makes 15 to 20 servings.

FLOURLESS CHOCOLATE CAKE

This rich, dense cake is the perfect choice for a fancy occasion.

12 oz. bittersweet or semisweet chocolate, chopped

¾ cup (1½ sticks) butter, sliced

6 eggs

¾ cup sugar

2 teaspoons vanilla

Fresh raspberries for garnish*

Powdered sugar for garnish

Butter the bottom of a 9-inch springform pan. Line with parchment, then butter the parchment paper. Cover the outside of the pan with foil. Preheat oven to 350 degrees.

In a medium saucepan over low heat, melt chocolate and butter, stirring it together. Cool, stirring occasionally.

Separate egg yolks from whites. In a large bowl, beat yolks with half the sugar for 3 minutes. Stir in chocolate mixture and vanilla. Set aside.

In a clean bowl, beat egg whites until they form soft peaks. Add remaining sugar, beating again until peaks are firm. Fold gently into chocolate batter and pour into springform pan. Bake 45-50 minutes, or until top puffs and cracks. Cool in pan.

Press sides of cake down to match sunken center. Run knife around edge. Remove sides of pan and invert onto serving platter. Peel off parchment. Cover with glaze (recipe below), pile high with fresh raspberries, and dust with powdered sugar.

Makes 12 servings.

* For a more elegant variation, dip the points of fresh strawberries in white or dark chocolate and arrange them point-side-up atop the cake.

GLAZE FOR FLOURLESS CHOCOLATE CAKE

½ cup whipping cream
½ cup corn syrup
9 oz. bittersweet or semisweet chocolate, grated

Simmer all ingredients in a medium saucepan until smooth; pour over cake. Chill 1 hour.

BUTTER PECAN CAKE

2⅔ cups chopped pecans
1¼ cups butter, softened and divided
2 cups sugar
4 eggs
3 cups flour
2 teaspoons baking powder
½ teaspoon salt   *(recipe continues)*

1 cup milk

2 teaspoons vanilla

Preheat oven to 350 degrees. Grease and flour *three* 9-inch cake pans. Place pecans and ¼ cup of butter in a rimmed baking sheet or pan. Bake for 20 minutes, stirring frequently. In a large bowl, beat sugar and remaining butter until fluffy. Add eggs one at a time, beating after each addition. Combine flour, baking powder, and salt. Add dry mixture to batter alternately with milk. Stir in vanilla and 1⅓ cups of the toasted pecans. Pour into three cake pans and bake for 25–30 minutes. Cool 10 minutes, then remove from pans to finish cooling on wire rack.

Frost (recipe below).

Makes 6 to 8 servings.

FROSTING FOR BUTTER PECAN CAKE

1 cup butter, softened

8 cups powdered sugar

1 (5 oz.) can evaporated milk

2 teaspoons vanilla

In a large bowl, cream butter with sugar. Add milk and vanilla, beating well. Stir in remaining pecans from cake recipe.

KILLER CHEESECAKE

This superlative cheesecake is the very best (it appears under various names), and can be topped with fruit or a fruit sauce.

2 cups graham cracker crumbs

½ cup (1 stick) butter, melted

3 tablespoons brown sugar

4 eggs

1¾ cups sugar

3 (8 oz.) packages cream cheese, softened

1 teaspoon vanilla

1 pint sour cream

Mix butter, crumbs, and brown sugar; press onto bottom of a 9-inch springform pan to form crust.

For filling, beat eggs and 1 cup sugar, then add cream cheese and vanilla. Beat thoroughly until glassy-smooth. Pour onto crust and bake at 350 degrees for 40 minutes. Cool. Beat sour cream and ¾ cup sugar to form topping; pour over cheesecake. Bake at 450 degrees for 10 minutes. Cool, then chill.

Makes 12 servings.

KEY LIME PIE

This is a common recipe, but so good that you need to have it in your repertoire. It also doubles well. (And try using lemon instead of lime!)

1 graham cracker crust, homemade or purchased

3 egg yolks, beaten (save the whites)

4 drops green food coloring

½ cup lime juice

1 (14 oz.) can sweetened condensed milk

Grated rind or curls of two limes

Whipped cream

With a mixer, beat yolks, food coloring, lime juice, and milk. Pour into crust. Bake at 350 degrees for 15 minutes; cool. Cover with whipped cream and lime curls. Chill. (You can make a meringue using the egg whites if you prefer, or save them for an egg-white omelette.)

Makes 6 servings.

MERINGUE FOR PIE

You'll want to know how to make a glossy meringue to dress up various pies. This one will cover a 9-inch pie.

3 egg whites
½ teaspoon cream of tartar
⅓ cup sugar

Beat egg whites with cream of tartar until soft peaks form, then add sugar and beat until fairly stiff with a satin sheen. (Note: When making meringue, make sure there are no specks of yolk or any oils in the bowl.) Spread meringue over pie in swirling motions, sealing edges against crust. Bake at 400 degrees for 10 minutes.

GANACHE

Ganache is a fabulous, thick frosting that works especially well as a thick filling between cake layers.

2 cups heavy cream
8 oz. semisweet or bittersweet chocolate, finely
   chopped

In a heavy pot, bring cream just to boiling; remove from heat. Add chocolate pieces and whisk until melted. Chill several hours, or several days. When ready to use, beat just until frosting is workable.

Makes enough for one cake.

LEMONADE TORTE

A no-cook treat that's perfect for hot summer days!

1¼ cups graham cracker crumbs
⅓ cup brown sugar

¼ cup melted butter

9 oz. frozen whipped topping, thawed

1 (6 oz.) can frozen lemonade

1 (14 oz.) can sweetened condensed milk

2 tablespoons lemon juice

In a small bowl, mix first three ingredients to form crust; press into bottom of 9-inch springform pan. Beat remaining ingredients until smooth and pour over crust. Chill 6 hours or overnight.

Makes 12 servings.

FUNNEL CAKES

These are fun to make for guests. None of us should eat deep-fried desserts every day, but on occasion it's fun to splurge.

Enough oil to measure 2 inches deep in your frying pan

2 eggs

1½ cups milk

2 cups flour

1 teaspoon baking powder

½ teaspoon salt

1 cup powdered sugar (sprinkled from a shaker or sifter if possible)

(recipe continues)

Heat oil until a bread cube sizzles (but not so hot that it smokes). Mix eggs, milk, flour, baking powder, and salt into a batter. Pour batter, in swirling motions and zigzags, through a funnel into the hot oil. It will look like a plate of spaghetti. When golden brown, remove with a spatula and drain on paper towels. Sprinkle generously with powdered sugar. Serve hot.

Makes 4 to 8 funnel cakes.

CHERRY CRISP

This is another common recipe, but so easy I had to include it.

2 cans cherry pie filling*
½ teaspoon cinnamon
¼ teaspoon almond extract
1 package white cake mix
½ cup (1 stick) butter, melted
½ cup chopped nuts (optional)

Preheat oven to 375 degrees. In a large bowl, mix pie filling, cinnamon, and extract. Pour into greased nine-by-thirteen-inch baking dish. Sprinkle with cake mix. Drizzle with butter and nuts. Bake for 35 minutes.

Makes 12 servings.

* Try it with apple pie filling, too!

CREAM CHEESE FROSTING

(This recipe can be halved for a smaller cake.)

2 (8 oz.) packages cream cheese, room temperature
½ lb. (2 sticks) butter, room temperature
4 cups powdered sugar

2 teaspoons orange juice

2 teaspoons grated orange rind (optional)

In a large bowl, whip cream cheese and butter until fluffy. Add remaining ingredients; mix until smooth.

Makes enough for 1 cake.

LEMON BARS

Don't be the only person you know who doesn't have this recipe!

Crust:

2 cups flour

1 cup butter, softened

½ cup powdered sugar

½ teaspoon salt

Filling:

4 eggs, beaten

2 cups granulated sugar

½ teaspoon baking powder

¼ cup flour

¼ cup lemon juice

2 cups powdered sugar

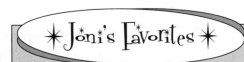

✳ Joni's Favorites ✳

Get to know your local baker and buy manufacturer's cream from him or her—it's much richer than cream sold in supermarkets and holds its shape better when whipped.

Preheat oven to 350 degrees. Cut crust ingredients together like pie dough. Press in bottom of nine-by-thirteen-inch baking pan. Bake 20 minutes. Meanwhile, combine eggs, granulated sugar, baking powder, flour, and lemon juice. Pour onto cooked crust. Return to oven and bake an additional 25 minutes. Remove from oven and sift powdered sugar over top. Cool; cut into squares.

Makes 15 to 20 servings.

PECAN BARS

Crust
3 cups flour
¼ cup sugar
½ teaspoon baking powder
½ teaspoon salt
½ cup shortening or lard
½ cup (1 stick) butter

Filling
1 cup brown sugar
1 cup butter (2 sticks)
¾ cup honey
½ cup sugar
¼ cup whipping cream
1 lb. (4 cups) crushed pecans
1 tablespoon vanilla

Preheat oven to 350 degrees. Grease a jelly-roll pan (cookie sheet with sides), then line with foil. In a large bowl, combine crust ingredients, cutting in shortening and butter like pie dough. Press onto bottom of jelly-roll pan. Bake until golden, about 15–20 minutes. While crust bakes, prepare filling. In a medium saucepan over high heat, bring sugars, butter, honey, and cream to boiling. Add pecans and vanilla. Pour mixture onto warm crust. Bake 30 minutes (it will firm as it cools). When cool, invert onto rack and peel off foil. Invert again to set right side up, then slice into squares.

Makes 15 to 20 servings.

FRUIT PIZZA

So simple, but such fun.

> 1 package refrigerated sugar cookie dough
> 1 (8 oz.) package cream cheese, softened
> ⅓ cup sugar
> 1 teaspoon vanilla
> 4 cups assorted fruit (blueberries, grapes, mandarin oranges, pineapple chunks, maraschino cherries, raspberries, peeled and sliced kiwi, sliced strawberries, etc.)

Slice cookie-dough roll into ¼-inch slices and place on a 12–14-inch pizza pan, covering pan. With moistened fingers, press slices together, forming a solid crust. Bake at 325 degrees for about 20 minutes, or until light tan. Cool.

In a large bowl, beat cream cheese, sugar, and vanilla. Spread over cooled crust. Decorate with fruit in pinwheel or circular pattern.

Makes 12 servings.

Joni's Favorites

A casserole dish holder is a necessity in my house. I find I am often taking nine-by-thirteen-inch baking dishes to sick neighbors, to potlucks, and to school and church events. It's handy to have a container with handles to carry hot dishes in, whether it's made of basket material, wood, or metal.

Cooking Terms

al dente: Italian, meaning "firm to the bite"—when pasta or vegetables are cooked tender-crisp

antipasto: Italian, meaning "before the pasta"—usually a tray of marinated vegetables, relishes, olives, and such

au gratin: a dish topped with cheese or bread crumbs

baste: to spoon liquid over meat periodically as it cooks

beat: to mix vigorously by hand, or with an electric mixer

bisque: a thick, creamy soup, usually featuring seafood

blanch: To immerse food briefly in boiling water (for example, to remove the skin of a peach)

bouillon: A concentrated broth flavoring, sold granulated or in cubes. Bouillon is also a clear broth-type soup.

bouquet garni: A cheesecloth package of herbs and seasonings that is immersed in a soup for flavoring, then removed

braise: To cook with moist heat, covered, after meat has browned

broil: To cook with direct, intense heat

caramelize: To cook slowly until sugar browns (onions can be caramelized with the sugar they naturally release)

chutney: A relish that's both spicy and sweet, originally East Indian

clarify: To melt fat so as to skim off the solids, as in clarifying butter

crimp: To pinch and seal pastry crusts together

crumb coat: The thin layer of frosting applied to a frozen cake to seal in crumbs and provide a smooth surface for final frosting

cube: To cut into one-half-inch size cubes

cut in: Using two knives and slicing crosswise through fat and flour to create a coarse mixture, such as required for pie dough. A pastry blender may also be used.

deglaze: To scrape bits of meat and other cooked bits from the roasting pan, usually for mixing into a sauce or gravy

dice: To cut food into one-quarter-inch sized (or smaller) cubes

en croute: Food cooked inside a pastry crust

fillet: To cut a piece of meat or fish so as to remove the bones

flambé: To light alcohol-doused foods

flash: A quick process, as in flash freezing produce right as it is picked, or "flashing" stale bread under water, then baking it to crisp it

fricasse: Stewed, braised meat in a white sauce

fry: To cook in oil on stove top (to deep fry means to immerse in hot oil)

galette: A rustic tart with hand-shaped edges, made from sweet tart dough

giblets: Poultry liver, neck, and heart, usually packaged inside the cavity of the bird. Used for making gravy, or cooked separately.

grease and flour: To coat (usually cake pans) with shortening then dust with flour

head space: The empty space allowed for food to expand when freezing in a container

invert: To turn a baked good out onto a cooling rack or serving tray upside down. If serving, first cover food with plate, then use pot holders to turn the entire combination over and remove the baking dish.

julienne: Vegetables cut into thin strips, matchstick size

knead: To work dough with one's hands in order to mix it thoroughly, distribute yeast throughout, and create elasticity. Generally, kneading is done by pressing the dough with the heel of the hand, folding it over, turning it, and repeating.

leavenings: Ingredients which make foods rise, such as yeast, baking powder, and baking soda

marinate: To soak meats, usually in the refrigerator, in a mixture that infuses flavor and increases tenderness

mince: To finely snip or chop into tiny particles

parboil: To precook in boiling water

pare: To cut away the peel

pipe: To press frosting or other soft food through a small hole in a pastry bag in order to make decorative trim

poach: To cook in liquid, slowly simmering

prosciutto: Italian, thinly sliced, smoked or spiced ham

puree: To whip or blend food into a smooth paste or thick sauce consistency

ramekins: Oven-proof pudding cups for individual crème brûlées, soufflés, etc.

reduce: To thicken a sauce, and reduce its volume, by cooking it longer and letting moisture steam off

rest: To allow meat to set for ten to fifteen minutes after cooking so that juices distribute evenly

roasting: To cook meat or vegetables with even, dry heat circulation

roulade: French, meaning "a rolling," usually referring to a meat or cake rolled around a filling

roux: A paste made from browned flour and fat, which forms the basis of many sauces and gravies, especially Cajun dishes

saturated fat: Fats containing cholesterol, such as animal fats and tropical oils. Unsaturated fats come from plants, such as corn and olive oil.

sauté: To cook food on the stove top, usually in a bit of oil, stirring frequently

sear: To quickly cook the exterior of meat or fish so that juices are sealed in

shred: To cut finely into threads, such as shredded cheese, or to pull apart into small bits, such as shredded chicken

sift: To allow dry ingredients, such as flour, to incorporate air by gently letting them fall through a fine mesh

simmer: To cook at low heat; without boiling

sliver: To slice thinly, such as slivered almonds

soft-ball stage: A stage of candy making when a sugar mixture has cooked to about 240 degrees and forms a soft ball when a small amount is dropped into cold water. Other stages are thread (230 degrees), firm-ball (245 degrees), hard-ball (255–260 degrees), and brittle (300 degrees).

spit roasting: To roast meat over coals, after securing it to a spit rod or rotisserie, then turning it for even cooking

steam: To allow food to cook by steam only, usually in a rack or metal basket above boiling water

stiff peaks: Upright points left when beaters are lifted from well-beaten cream or meringue

stir-fry: To cook quickly, stirring constantly, over high heat, usually with a bit of oil

stock: The liquid used to boil meat or vegetables; a seasoned broth used for making soups and other dishes

tempering chocolate: Maintaining the proper gloss and texture during candy making by keeping melted chocolate at 86–91 degrees. Also prevents chalky or waxy results.

truss: To tie the legs of poultry together before cooking

vent: To pierce the top crust of a pie so steam can escape

vinaigrette: A salad dressing made with oil, vinegar, and spices

whisk: To whip briskly with a wire whisk

wrap: A sandwich "wrapped" in a tortilla or other thin food, such as a lettuce leaf or a wonton wrapper

zest: The outer, colored part of citrus skin

Index

279